JOCHEN RINDT

JOCHEN RINDT

The Story of a World Champion

by

HEINZ PRÜLLER

in collaboration with
JOCHEN RINDT

WILLIAM KIMBER
LONDON

First published in England in 1971 by
WILLIAM KIMBER & CO. LIMITED
Godolphin House, 22a Queen Anne's Gate, London, S.W.1

First Impression June 1971
Second Impression January 1972

© Heinz Prüller, 1970
SBN 7183 0162 5

This book is copyright. No part of it may be reproduced in any form without permission in writing from the publishers except by a reviewer who wishes to quote brief passages in connection with a review written for inclusion in a magazine or newspaper or a radio broadcast

Translated from the German
by
PETER EASTON

MADE AND PRINTED IN GREAT BRITAIN BY PURNELL AND SONS, LTD.
PAULTON (SOMERSET) AND LONDON

Contents

Chapter		Page
	Introduction by Jackie Stewart	11
1	The Ten Thousand Pound Promise	19
2	The Wild Ones from Graz	22
3	'Unknown Australian Beats Hill'	28
4	The 21-hour Grand Prix of Le Mans	32
5	The Cooper Period	37
6	No Car Killer	45
7	The Formula 2 Classics	48
8	Nina	55
9	'Black Jack'	62
10	'The Line between Success and Disaster is Very Thin'	65
11	Under Brabham's Wing	70
12	Ford Intervenes	78
13	The Secret Grand Prix: Why Lotus?	84
14	Levin—An Upside Down Start	89
15	Barcelona	95
16	Mr Motor Racing—Colin Chapman	101
17	Decision for Lotus	110
18	Watkins Glen: Jochen at Last	117
19	Show Time	121

Chapter		Page
20	Kyalami: Imperfect Paradise	127
21	Lotus 72	132
22	Jarama: the Shorn Lotus Blossom	134
23	Monaco, his Biggest Success	140
24	More than a Lifespan	149
25	Zandvoort: the Muted Victory	155
26	Clermont-Ferrand — a Win from Third Place	162
27	Brands Hatch: Two Failures, Two Successes	170
28	Hockenheim: for Jimmy, the Last Garland	178
29	Five Weeks	185
30	September 4th	191
31	September 5th	197
32	Epilogue at Watkins Glen	203

Illustrations

	Facing Page
Jochen Rindt at Zeltweg, 1970	16
Jochen Rindt	17
Rindt wins from Graham Hill, Crystal Palace, 1964	32
Rindt wins from Jimmy Clark, Reims, 1965	32
The start of a Formula 2 race	33
Masten Gregory and Jochen Rindt after their victory at Le Mans, 1965	48
Jochen battling with Guichet during the Le Mans 24-hour Race, 1965	48
Rindt's Cooper-Maserati during practice for the German Grand Prix, Nürburgring, 1966	49
Pit signal: Jochen leads a Grand Prix for the first time; the Cooper-Maserati at Spa, 1966	49
Jochen driving the Brabham, Nürburgring, 1968	64
The Rindt Lotus spins into the banking at Indianapolis 1969 (sequence of four photographs)	65
Water skiing	80
And just skiing	80
The wedding, Helsinki, 5th March, 1967	81
The Jochen Rindt Show, Vienna	81
Jochen's Lotus takes off during the Spanish Grand Prix at Barcelona, 4th May, 1969	96
Barcelona, 1969: Jochen's car hurtles towards the remains of Graham Hill's car	97
Graham Hill trying to extricate Rindt	97
Spanish police by the wreckage of the two cars	97
Jochen and Nina in Switzerland	112
Flying Lotus 49: Nürburgring, 1969	113

Illustrations

Rindt in the cockpit: Clermont Ferrand, 1969	113
Natascha's second birthday	128
Waiting in the paddock (sequence of four photographs)	129
In the pits at Zandvoort, 1969	144
The Lotus team: Colin Chapman with mechanics Eddie and Herbie behind him	144
Maurice Phillippe and the world championship winning Lotus 72	145
Monte Carlo, 1970: Rindt takes Pescarolo and the chase after Brabham begins	160
Piers Courage with his son Jason	161
The start of the Belgian Grand Prix, Spa, 1970. Chris Amon's March leading from Jochen's Lotus 49	161
The first lap at Zandvoort in 1970: Jacky Ickx (Ferrari) in front of Jochen (Lotus 72)	176
Jochen after winning the Dutch Grand Prix at Zandvoort, 1970	176
Jochen's fourth Grand Prix victory: Clermont Ferrand, 1970, with Chris Amon in pursuit	177
The lucky victor: Rindt leads Brabham at Brands Hatch: the British Grand Prix, 1970	177
Hockenheim and Jochen's last victory: the German Grand Prix, 1970	192
Jochen Rindt and Colin Chapman	192
The lake at Geneva	193
Graz, 11th September, 1970: Graham Hill and Jack Brabham	193

Acknowledgements for the use of copyright illustrations are due to the following: Uwe Berger (1), Bernard Cahier (1), Pascal Ickx (1), Ferdi Krähling (5), Leal (1), Patrick Lichfield (1), Markeson (2), Lynton Money (1), Photo Actualites (1), Reinhard (4), A. H. Rottensteiner (9), Milan Schijatschky (2), Lucky Schmidleitner (5), Sven Simson (1), Vulkaistavaski (1), Jim Winslow (3), John Wright (1).

After Clermont Ferrand, when Jochen for the first time was in the lead of the Championship, Jochen and Heinz agreed to start on their second book. The first book they made 4 years ago.

I am very happy Heinz is doing this book, which is the only book which has been agreed on by both Jochen and myself.

Because Heinz was not only a journalist but also a very close friend of us, and with the help of some of our friends, I am sure this book will be the most true story about Jochen, and his life.

I hope all the friends & fans of Jochen will like it, I know I will.

Nina

FOR NINA

INTRODUCTION
Jackie Stewart

Jochen was one of the most sincere men that I ever knew. He was absolutely honest in all his convictions. He really truly felt the things he said. He was a man who upset almost as many people as he became friends with. He was a tremendously hard man, and if he had no time for someone he would not give them any time. He would not put a face on something when he didn't want to do it. I can think of one particular person he did not like at all—not for anything he had done to Jochen but for what he stood for and the way he conducted his life. I can remember a number of occasions when I was talking to this man; Jochen would come up and neither address him nor acknowledge his presence. He would start a conversation with me without even recognising the man. He would not even say good afternoon or pass the time of day. This is something that I admired tremendously about Jochen. Once he had made his decision and had classified someone he completely abided by his judgement. He was not swayed by other people saying, 'Jochen you have to do this,' or 'Jochen why don't you do that?' Jochen had made up his mind and that was that. This was clear in everything he did—in the way he lived his life. If he chose to be friendly with someone he was friendly with them and he admired them and he liked them. If he thought someone was a fool he regarded him as a complete fool and gave him no opportunity to win back his respect. Therefore I felt that this book—even more than the one

Jochen Rindt

Jochen and Heinz wrote in 1966 — would be a true and honest account of his views and his life in motor racing.

Since 1966 Jochen had matured tremendously as a man. He had become more rounded and a little bit more mellow. He was also slightly more willing to come and go in the things that were of minor importance, but yet surrounded his existence. He had matured even more as a driver, because in the last eighteen months of his life he had come away from the point of having to win races. Before that, I think, he had tried terribly hard to win races. He had done everything in his power to win a Grand Prix. He desperately wanted to win a Grand Prix. But after he had won one he realised it was not all that difficult. It is like a lot of other things in life. Your goal seems impossible until you achieve it, but once you have achieved it it comes very easily to you. So when he won at Watkins Glen in 1969, I for one recognised that this was not going to be the only Grand Prix he would win. And then, of course, he went on to win five more in quick succession in 1970; I think this was partly due to the fact that he no longer drove as hard as he had done; previously he had felt that he had to justify his presence as a driver. I am sure that in the last few races Jochen did he drove easily; without a great deal of effort, without having to push very hard. Of course, when you are winning, generally it is not very difficult. It's easy to win but it's difficult to lose. You have to drive very hard to be second or third. But when you are winning a race you seldom have to drive flat out the whole way. There are very few races in which a top Grand Prix driver has to really extend himself for the entire distance. I don't think that Jochen did in Monte Carlo. He said he did but I don't think he did; I think his assessment was coloured by the effort which he put into the last quarter of the race; I am sure he did not drive that hard in the first quarter of the race. But his performance there was very good. He found himself in a position to win after a few problems had befallen other people, but he took his opportunity and he used it to the

Introduction by Jackie Stewart

fullest of his ability—and, of course, he won the race. He drove hard in the British Grand Prix—he was pushed all the way by Jack Brabham—but the other wins came more easily; Jochen felt that he had the best car and therefore drove in a manner that would conserve it. It was in things like this that he had matured most, but I think that his whole life had taken on a slightly different colour. He was less intense. He became more relaxed. This showed not only in the way he came down to my home and relaxed more easily than I had seen him do before, but also in the way he relaxed much more in a racing car—and therefore gave the car an easier time. I think this is the thing I noticed more than anything else about Jochen in 1970.

It goes without saying that I regarded Jochen as a real competitor. Since the time when Jim Clark died, Jochen was one of the very few men I really felt I had totally to compete against. He was the one man I was always aware of. There were other drivers who on some days went fast, but I always felt that Jochen was the man most likely to beat me. Throughout our racing lives together we had a lot of really good battles. The two which are most clear in my mind are the Formula 2 race at Karlskoga in 1967, when we raced for a while with Jimmy and then went ahead of him and had the most monumental battle—passing and repassing, carving each other up—and the other was the 1969 British Grand Prix. We both drove very hard that day—we were both right on the limit I think—and it was a very close race until we got involved with some traffic and Jochen pulled out a two- or three-second lead. I had to drive at my absolute limit to prevent him getting further away, and he had to do the same to maintain his lead. Then he had trouble—part of his rear aerofoil came loose and was touching a tyre—so he had to stop at the pits, and later he had to stop again to refuel; as a result of this I was able to ease off and win the race quite comfortably.

Jochen and I respected each other because of the big

battles we had. We had another very close race at Monza in 1969. This was a tremendous battle in which we were wheel to wheel for the entire distance. We both led the race more often than anyone else and we both understood each other very well. Once again I won and Jochen came second, but the gap at the finish was only a matter of inches.

The thing I most enjoyed about our racing experiences together was our mutual understanding. There are very few people you can trust implicitly in a racing car; Jim Clark was one of them. Dan Gurney, for me, was another. And Jochen came into the same category in that I always felt I could communicate with him during a race. We would never, at any time, use tactics against each other which were in any way questionable. I cannot remember Jochen saying to me, or my having to say to him: 'For Christ's sake, you put one in a jam there'; it just never happened. Either I let him through knowing that he had put me in an embarrassing position, or he gave way to me. We never went into a corner hard-headed, waiting to see who would chicken out first; we both realised that this would only waste time. We both recognised that when we went into the lead at Monza together, the chances were that we would be able to handle the rest of the opposition.

There was another classic example at Reims. On the starting grid we said to each other: 'Right. When the flag drops we both take off and stay alongside each other. You lead into the first corner and I will lead into the second.' By doing this we were able to hold up people behind us whom we were scared of, not physically scared of, but people we didn't want to get involved with because they could use dangerous tactics. Even when it came to the last lap the same protocol applied. Even when it was a matter of win or lose, we never lost our respect for each other. I cannot remember him doing anything that would have screwed me up, nor do I think I ever did the dirty on him. That just would not have happened. It was not that we were being

Introduction by Jackie Stewart

gentlemen; it was simply that we respected each other's talent. This is something that I am going to miss enormously. I had this sort of communication only a little time with Jimmy because I had neither the experience nor the machinery to allow me to compete with him.

Anyway, Jochen's ability as a driver for me is unquestioned. There are only two drivers I have driven against who I consider truly great; Jimmy and Jochen. They are the only two people I have had complete respect for. And I respected Jochen all the more because I grew up with him. When I started racing against Jimmy it was something I was coming into. I was the new boy and I was looking up to him. Jochen and I came in together and progressed together. My particular set of circumstances was luckier than Jochen's. I had better machinery in my early Formula 1 days than Jochen did. But latterly he had blossomed into being the number one Lotus driver, which meant that he was going to be the number one challenger. To make comparisons with other great drivers is very difficult for me — very difficult for anyone. But I would say that Jochen must rank very high from a driver's point of view. He was a driver's driver, like a man being a man's man. He went quickly in practice; he went smoothly; he had a tremendous amount of aggressiveness in his driving but he also had intelligence. He was the only driver I was happy to race with in the opening laps. Most drivers get very excited at the start of a race, and sometimes it takes them several laps to adjust. Jochen was completely switched on from the moment the flag dropped.

I don't think the accident at Monza was due to driver error. It was just fate. When something like this happens it is all the more saddening because you know there is nothing the driver can do. It is something that happens in a split second. You apply the brakes or you change down or you turn the steering wheel and something goes wrong. When this happens you cease to be the driver and become a passenger. Until this time you have been the master of your car, in

Jochen Rindt

complete control of everything around you. You know that you can do almost anything with the car; you can place it on the same mark on the road every lap. But when something goes wrong you are no longer the master, you are just along for the ride. And when that happens, whether it is because of a car problem, an oil leak or aquaplaning, there is nothing you can do about it. You could crash into a barrier, or you could spin all the way through a series of corners without hitting anything.

In 1966, going through the Masta Kink at Spa, Jochen spun on the same river that I spun on. He spun all the way through the Masta Kink, through the left hander; through the right hander; ended up facing the wrong way; put his foot on the throttle and spun round again. He was doing 170 miles an hour and he did not hit a thing. I once spun between two bridge parapets at Watkins Glen. I was doing 140 mph at the time, and I cannot conceive how I spun in such a limited space and did not hit anything. The car never even stopped. It was pointing in the right direction so I selected a gear and off I went. I thought about it afterwards. I did not go home and say 'Jesus, I really controlled that.' I did nothing, I was a puppet on a string, and somebody else was pulling the strings. At Monza Jochen had thirty or forty feet of track and grass to spin on. He could have spun off on either side and not hit anything. Instead of which he hit a barrier — a barrier that was in the safest place imaginable. But he hit it at a hundred and eighty miles an hour. And when something of this kind happens the outcome is just a matter of luck. If you hit the barrier the right way you get away with it; the car is damaged but you step out unhurt. Jochen didn't hit it the right way; he hit it at the base of an upright. It is only a matter of inches we are talking about, and this is the most dreadful thing of all.

Monza must be one of the world's safest tracks now. It is not entirely safe because of speed, but you never can eliminate speed; that is what motor racing is all about. But

Jochen Rindt at Zeltweg, 1970

Jochen Rindt

Introduction by Jackie Stewart

we had all the barriers, all the fences and all the run off areas that we wanted. We felt that it was as safe as it could possibly be made at that time. Yet it still claimed a life.

The thing I wanted most, after Jochen died, was to be sure that he won the world championship. At one time there was a doubt whether it would be awarded to him, even if nobody else surpassed his points total. I felt very strongly that it should be awarded to him; I could not imagine anyone taking this honour away; it really would have been a terrible thing. And rightly, the award was given to him. I think Jochen was a truly great world champion. He became champion in a convincing way, against very stiff opposition. I am sure that if he had lived he would have won two if not three more Grands Prix last year. I think he would have won Monza, Canada and America — that's three straight away — and if he had done this he would have collected a lot more points than he actually did. And if Jochen had lived Ferrari would not have dominated the last few races in the way that they did. For all these reasons I feel that the 1970 world championship went to the finest driver of 1970: therefore it was awarded correctly.

Whether Jochen had won any more races or not, everyone would have acclaimed him as the true 1970 world champion. I think he would have stayed on with Team Lotus for 1971, and I am sure he would have been a major force to be reckoned with again. Whatever other cars or drivers there are, it takes quite a while to build up the knowledge, experience and confidence that Jochen had just discovered. So I think he would have continued to be the driver to beat in 1971. One or two of us might have had better cars, which would have enabled us to offer him more opposition, but the biggest problem for all of us would have been to beat Jochen.

Begnins; October 12 1970.

CHAPTER ONE

The Ten Thousand Pound Promise

First of all I want to congratulate you on your win in Canada, wrote Nina Rindt in mid-October in a letter to Jacky Ickx. *To be honest: I was a little worried that you might win Watkins Glen and Mexico City as well, which would have meant that Jochen had lost the championship. I am very happy Jochen managed it after all; it was his only burning wish.*

If he stays alive, he will become World Champion: that's what they had said about the 'young wild one' at the beginning of his career. He did not survive this most demanding of sports, which is so unforgiving. But he became World Champion in 1970, the first German-speaking one and the twelfth in the roll of great names, of whom seven are still alive. And of these he was the only one to die in a Formula 1 racing car.

Since Monza, Nina Rindt has received well over a thousand letters. Alice Caracciola sent her a collection of press cuttings *because I was grateful that someone collected them for me when Rudi died.* Graham Hill forwarded a letter from the great train robber, Roy James, written from his Isle of Wight prison cell in a beautifully formal style. *He apologises for the prison paper,* added Graham.

From Italy a photo arrived: Clay Regazzoni had won the Jochen Rindt memorial trophy at Imola. Trophies didn't bother Jochen. Only four of them remain to commemorate his six Grand Prix victories: Watkins Glen, Monaco,

Jochen Rindt

Clermont-Ferrand and Hockenheim. The rest were kept by Lotus; his laurel wreaths he gave to the mechanics.

In Jochen's study at Begnins, near Geneva in Switzerland, above the typewriter, the steering wheel ashtray and the adding machine, there is a mounted photo of the wet and foggy Nürburgring race of 1968, in which he put up one of his best performances while with the Brabham team. On another wall there is a photo of Jochen in the cockpit of a Lotus, with Colin Chapman squatting alongside. Scribbled underneath are the words *Let us hope, Jochen, that 1970 will be your year! Colin.*

My diary notes for November 14th 1969 report a long evening with Jochen. We sat in a typical Viennese *Heurigen* tavern with the orchestra parodying an old music-hall melody with its traditional tragi-comic ending. There followed general laughter, but Jochen remained serious: 'I don't find that funny.'

At the forty-eighth attempt he had finally won his first Grand Prix, at Watkins Glen, and he had signed again with Lotus for 1970.

'I want to be World Champion next year, and with it the biggest name in motoring,' confided Jochen. 'But racing will only be one chapter of my life, and once I become World Champion I want to retire. I don't intend to be burnt out by the time I'm thirty, and only continue because I can't do, or don't know, anything else. There are so many things I want to do.'

'Once you are World Champion, wouldn't you want to try to join the ranks of the greatest of all time, like Jimmy Clark with his record of twenty-five Grand Prix victories?'

'Look where Jimmy is,' snorted Jochen.

'And your one Grand Prix success in Watkins Glen — quite an achievement when all is said and done; isn't that enough?'

'No, because I have to prove something.'

'That you are the best in the world?'

'Yes. Actually there are only two top-rank professionals:

The Ten Thousand Pound Promise

Stewart and I. Because we drive with our heads.'

Rindt, one of the most intelligent racing drivers of all time, tried to judge the risks involved: 'The chance of buying it' — Jochen's Austrian way of describing this eventuality is quite untranslatable — 'is always there. It is merely a matter of luck whether I pull through or not. You were in Barcelona and saw the crash; yet I won the next race I drove in, at Zolder. Not many other drivers would have managed that. And I have been racing now for eight years. Very few people can imagine what it means — eight years of race driving!'

He had a drink, and he smoked as he went on: 'I want to live, I could live from my Racing Car Show alone,' and then he repeated it all. Jochen spoke softly, with conviction and absolute confidence.

There had been hints of racing fatigue during the previous winters when Jochen had said: 'No one can assess just what it means to participate in Grand Prix racing, what it means in physical and mental strain.' Whenever he went off on a skiing holiday he used to observe: 'At the moment I can't imagine sitting in a racing car.' But the nearer the next racing season approached the more he missed his racing, and the more it became clear to him how keen a racing driver he really was.

His promise of November 14th 1969 was a serious one, and he didn't attempt to amend it until August 1970. A few days later Nina confirmed to me: 'Jochen has promised me that, if he becomes World Champion and continues driving, he will give me £10,000.' It would be fair to accept this in good faith. Rindt had a keen business sense and was unlikely to risk such a sum, although he used to remark: 'The only one who is going to become a millionaire through his racing is Stewart. Not me.'

CHAPTER TWO

The Wild Ones From Graz

Scotsman Jackie Stewart drove cars which belonged to others right from the very beginning; Jochen Rindt bought his own. The money came from the family firm of Klein & Rindt, a spice mill which was founded in 1840. Both Jochen's parents were killed in the summer of 1943 during a bombing raid on Hamburg; he became an orphan at fifteen months. Until he came of age the spice works was administered by his guardians.

In the meantime his days in Graz in southern Austria were wild and somewhat irresponsible. During this time his competitive spirit, his desire to go one better, grew. Admittedly his enthusiasm for academic subjects was little greater than that of Jacky Ickx ('Belgium's worst scholar'), but he was just as keen on sports as Jackie Stewart. 'I was always the best tennis player and skier in my class,' Jochen claimed. In the downhill race for the provincial school championships he broke his foot; experiences which the rather delicate Scottish schoolboy Stewart, nicknamed Chickenbones, who once missed 86 schooldays because of illness, was to encounter even more often.

Jochen's first 'sponsor' was a policeman living in his grandparents' house who owned a moped. The fifteen-year-old Jochen managed to convince the policeman he was sixteen, and used the moped regularly until he got his own. Thus commenced his motoring competition. With his friends Helmut Marko, the son of an electrical dealer; Andy Zahl-

The Wild Ones from Graz

bruckner, a local doctor's son; Stefan Pachanek, who was to become a six-day trials rider later on; and Helmut Reininghaus of the brewing dynasty of the same name, Jochen battled in bitter Moto-Cross contests. 'Those mopeds were good for nearly 50 mph and we got hurt practically every Sunday.'

Jochen's grandfather, Dr Hugo Martinowitz, a highly respected solicitor, had great difficulties in fending off threats of police action. Then Jochen collided with his chemistry professor, resulting in his speedy departure from the Pestalozzi School. At his next school Jochen's sojourn was even shorter because he sabotaged a Getting-to-know-Vienna excursion. In desperation, his grandparents sent him to Chichester as an exchange student, so that he could at least learn English, under the supervision of a retired army officer. So it is quite untrue that the first words he learnt in England were 'starting money', as British journalists were later to claim.

Jochen remembered spending one boring Saturday afternoon at the Goodwood racing circuit; he much preferred to go sailing. Returning to Austria, he was sent to a private school at Bad Aussee, where he ran into his old moped friends. The day before his eighteenth birthday, when he would finally be able to take his driving test, he was on the ski slopes. 'I'll risk nothing, I'll take it very easy,' he said — and promptly broke his foot for the second time in the difficult spring snow.

To help him get to school the spice works lent him an old Volkswagen which stank of pepper, complete with German number plates and chauffeur. But it was not long before Jochen fired the chauffeur, preferring to drive himself in spite of his plaster cast.

The car opened up magnificent new competitive possibilities. Four up, they drove off. The driver must ensure he changed gear at maximum revs and took every corner on the limit. If the other three decided the performance fell short of perfection, or if the car spun or overturned, another driver would take over.

In time for his holidays Jochen got a Simca Montlhéry. The intention was that he should drive his grandparents around in it, but in fact it was used to establish near-records between Graz and Bruck. During the night Marko brought out his parents' Chevrolet; they managed to stop and divert other traffic with vague explanations of 'official test driving'. Because Rindt's car was slower, Marko was not permitted to overtake on the few straights but only on corners. This he tried, but unfortunately encountered an unexpected lorry. The Chevy skidded across the road and balanced on the edge of a precipice. In despair, Marko tried to push the car, but instead of rolling back into the road it slithered down the slope.

'That's how he won,' recounts Marko. 'In those years, although we belonged to the same gang, we weren't very considerate to each other. We couldn't afford to be oversensitive, as this was regarded as a weakness and any weakness was taken advantage of. If one of us got into difficulties, no one helped him. We just watched to see how he would cope. To ask for help would have been entirely against our own rules.'

The 'gang' was not highly regarded in Graz; Jochen, with his wild hair-style and his perennial blue jeans, was notorious, according to Marko. 'Others of our age were not allowed to associate with us.'

Jochen never tired of organizing new forms of motoring competitions, and one of the sports he dreamed up involved towing a sledge. The person who could hold on longest was the winner. 'Forty-five mph isn't bad, and we always have a really good Saturday programme,' Rindt declared.

Next they tried skijoring, being pulled along on skis by a car. Unfortunately Jochen collided with a buried snowplough and his Simca was virtually split in two.

All these 'speed trials' on the country roads near Graz

The Wild Ones from Graz

resulted in new records. Many years later, when Jochen was driving in Grand Prix events and Marko was engaged in Formula Vee racing, Jochen would shake his head in disbelief: 'Can you understand it, Helmut? I simply cannot equal our old times any longer even though I drive faster cars and I drive better.' Marko has experienced the same phenomenon.

In 1961, Rindt and Marko decided to drive to the German Grand Prix at the Nürburgring. Jochen left his wallet behind and they reached Mainz without money and with an empty petrol tank. The night porter at the spice works refused to let them in. 'Don't be so silly, the factory belongs to me,' insisted a furious Jochen. Finally they managed to rouse a secretary, and she advanced some cash. Because of this they missed the start of the race, but arrived at the Karussell in time to see Moss triumph over von Trips and Phil Hill.

Count von Trips, who appeared all set for the 1961 world championship, became the idol of the gang, partly because he was German-speaking and partly because the motoring magazines said he was the top German driver. On September 10th Rindt and Marko saw the huge headlines as they returned to Graz from a hill climb: *Trips killed at Monza.* One of their friends saw the accident as the cars went into the Parabolica and reported in detail. 'We were downcast, but other than a certain amount of hero worship, little remained,' says Marko.

Their own ambitions eventually led them from their wild but illicit activities to proper organized events. Rindt in his Simca, Marko in a borrowed Steyr Puch, and Pachanek on a Honda motor-cycle which cost the princely sum of £5, entered for the Styrian Mountain Rally. Then they went to a race at Innsbruck. Udo Poschmann, the former secretary of the Austrian Automobile Sports Club, remembers it clearly: 'A former champion sold his Rally-Simca to some toff in Graz, and promised him an entry in the touring car race at Innsbruck Airport.' When the toff arrived to sign on he had a wild hair-do and was wearing odd lengths of string instead

Jochen Rindt

of shoe-laces. Poschmann was shocked, but let him enter. Rindt finished third, right up among the Alfas.

Early in 1962 Jochen became the last member of the gang to pass his exams. It almost seemed as if they were settling down at last. Marko was going to read law, and Jochen was accepted at the Vienna Polytechnic for World Trade. But his first lecture was also his last. The blame for this can be attributed to an Alfa Romeo Giulietta TI, duly modded by Conrero in Turin at the expense of his grandmother. Rindt went from success to success with this car, but his friends told him he might not find things quite so easy in Italy. However, he managed to defeat the Italians, too, and this finally pointed the way ahead.

'It seems evident I have some talent, so I shouldn't waste my time in small events any longer,' Jochen decided. 'It wouldn't be fair to the others to continually collect laurel wreaths, no matter how unimportant the races. We all have to start competing as a hobby. Some want to take it further, but not the majority. For one thing they don't have the time or the capability; for others it's simply too dangerous.' Jochen recognised all this in 1962 and arranged his life accordingly.

For the 1963 season he acquired Kurt Barry's Formula Junior Cooper, though he wasn't able to pay for it until his twenty-first birthday. He really needed a guardian angel to pass from touring cars to single-seaters without a major accident, but he summed it up himself by saying 'I was just lucky'. He made his Formula Junior debut at Vallelunga in Italy, where he caused a sensation by recording the fastest practice time. The next race he won, overtaking the Italian Geki Russo (and an ambulance which happened to be on the track) in a hair-raising manner. Russo's team manager de Sanctis was impressed: 'That fellow Rindt has world class,' he said. 'He has the right face for a successful driver – flat cheekbones and slit eyes.'

Later, on the pavé of Budapest, Rindt lost control at

The Wild Ones From Graz

over 90 mph when he hit a large puddle, and only just avoided skidding into the packed spectators. After Monte Carlo, Piers Courage, then an up-and-coming driver, told his friend Frank Williams: 'Jochen Rindt—to me that means a red and white polka dot silk scarf, pink trousers and an E-type Jaguar; in other words, a snob.' As Piers circulated in pretty elevated circles himself, Jochen came to much the same conclusions about his later friend!

Frank Williams watched the new 'wonder boy' for a couple of races and then introduced himself: 'From now on you have a new fan.' In practice at the Nürburgring, Jochen waved to Frank walking back to the pits. Next time round he ran off the road when a slower driver obstructed his line. Undismayed he told Frank to jump on the back of the crumpled Cooper and drove back to the pits at over 60 mph, although according to Frank the wheels looked like falling off at any moment. Briefly in hospital at Adenau, Jochen thought of giving it all up 'because my nerves won't stand it'. But he didn't think that way for long.

'It was in 1963 that I recognised motor racing suited me better than anything else. This discovery pleased me, because otherwise I would have wasted two years.' I once asked him how often in those days he drove beyond his limits. 'Did I ever drive within them?' he countered.

CHAPTER THREE

'Unknown Australian Beats Hill'

Being able to buy a Formula 2 Brabham at the age of twenty-two is perhaps not altogether unknown. But to win with it one's second race, and in England at that, was unheard of, at least until Jochen came along. But first he made his appearance at the 1964 Racing Car Show wearing a camelhair coat and looking extremely wealthy, according to Frank Williams. The object of the visit was to pay Jack Brabham a cool £4,000. He stayed in the famous flat shared by Frank and Jonathan Williams, Piers Courage, Charles Lucas and Charlie Crichton-Stuart. He even acquired a mechanic.

Came Whitsun and a busy weekend, with races at both Mallory Park and Crystal Palace. At Mallory Park Jochen asked Denny Hulme if he could follow him for a lap because the track was an unknown quantity to him. Denny, always helpful, nodded in agreement and promptly enabled Rindt to take pole position. He was even faster than Jimmy Clark, just returned from qualifying at Indianapolis.

On the sidelines for once, Jackie Stewart, then the Formula 3 star of the year, watched the start. He was surprised to see an unfamiliar blue car in pole position and said of the driver: 'He looks very young, like a schoolboy, lost and somewhat out of place. His helmet doesn't seem to fit him and I can't quite see how he made fastest time. An Austrian in England . . . must be a timing error.'

There was no error, but at the start of the race Jochen was not in gear—and was last away. Fighting his way up

'Unknown Australian Beats Hill'

through the field, he became involved in a massive incident that affected half the runners, but he still finished third behind Clark and Arundell.

Jackie Stewart kept an eye on Rindt as being the only new face worthy of his attention. He realised here was a future threat, so he took a closer look in the paddock. Not appreciating Jochen's Austrian background, he analysed the new driver for me as follows: 'He squats in front of his transporter and looks as if he couldn't care less whether anyone talks to him or not. He obviously wants to be independent and asks no-one for any favours; a bit of a "loner", perhaps. A man who doesn't need any help and who doesn't want anyone to think he does.'

Next day the Crystal Palace meeting started with two heats. Graham Hill won the heat of the experts in front of Clark and Hulme; Rindt the heat of the amateurs from Rees and Ahrens. Rindt was only two-tenths of a second slower than Hill; Rees, the king of Crystal Palace, where he had an enviable reputation, registered astonishment: 'I intended to pass Jochen at South Tower corner, but he just moved over to the right and stayed in front!'

At the start of the final Hill asked his mechanic the name of the boy with the unruly hair. As soon as the forty-lap race began, the boy with the unruly hair filled Graham's mirrors. 'That dark blue Brabham was sideways throughout the race; it left the corners at unbelievable angles and always looked as if it was about to go off the road,' Robin Herd, then better known as an aircraft designer, told his old school friend Alan Rees.

Clark dropped out. Twice the wheels of Rindt's and Hill's cars touched. Rindt's hands were blistered as a result of constant gear changing. The soles of his feet hurt him. But on lap 15 he got past Hill—whose rear anti-roll bar had broken—and went on to win. *Unknown Australian beats Graham Hill* splashed the headline of a London newspaper the next day, obviously believing that all the best racing drivers come from the Dominions. 'I think I've made it,' Jochen told me, 'and BP has raised my contract money to such an extent I thought I was dreaming.'

Denis Druitt, competitions manager of BP immediately took to Jochen personally when he visited him in his office after Crystal Palace. Druitt recognised at once: this was a man on his way up. The contract was quickly amended from its old level of £25 per race to £1,200 for the season.

For the rest of 1964 Jochen battled on as lone wolf against the works Formula 2 cars, but realised it was better to fight his future rivals on equal terms instead of trying to make the running in Formula 1 with an outclassed machine. Jochen also learnt to classify the top drivers. 'Jimmy Clark is so quick that he doesn't need to fight it out with the others. But if he does get mixed up with the pack, then there's no one who looks in his mirror as often as he. I always feel safe racing with Jimmy. The same with Graham; although he fights it out to the last, I know he would never play a dirty trick. He drives hard but I feel the way he does.'

At Reims Jochen was only sixty feet behind Ginther and Arundell when their cars touched; Arundell's Lotus somersaulted several times and broke up, while its engine cowling hit Rindt's car. He stopped at once and dived through the dust cloud to go to Arundell's assistance. Back in the pits Jochen declared he had lost the desire to go on. He was told off. 'I didn't know at that time that one must stay in the race as long as one's car is half-way driveable. You just don't stop on the track. This is the sort of mistake only a beginner makes.'

Bang in the middle of the season, Rindt lost his mechanic and for the rest of the year Jochen had to manage with a badly prepared car, but he remained consistently quick and the people who matter in motor racing began to take notice.

Jochen made his Formula 1 debut in the 1964 Austrian Grand Prix at Zeltweg Airfield, driving a Brabham-BRM entered by Rob Walker. Photographers were at the airport as the top drivers arrived and tried to arrange the classic, handshaking photographs—Rindt and Clark, then Rindt with Hill—but Jochen was determined to avoid being obtrusive; he didn't yet feel like master in his own home, but more like a guest in his own country.

The drivers' briefing was held in English and Jochen missed a point. When he asked, one of the English drivers turned round and suggested: 'Don't worry, just follow us.' For Rindt there seemed a hope of world championship points, but brake trouble forced him into the pits and later the steering failed.

But Rob Walker was satisfied. Later that year Jochen phoned him several times to see if he could fix up a Formula 1 contract, but Walker faced a difficulty in that Jochen was signed up with BP. In addition Denis Druitt had already started negotiations with Cooper. . . .

Six years later Jochen asked the man who gave him his first Formula 1 opportunity: 'Tell me, Rob, was it really only the BP link with Cooper that decided you to turn me down?' Walker replied frankly: 'I couldn't have guaranteed you any starting places, as Cooper could.'

In 1970 Rob Walker wrote in the American magazine *Road and Track*: 'The greater Jochen's successes, the nicer a person he becomes.' This remark followed the Austrian Grand Prix at the new Österreichring, situated only two kilometres away from the old Zeltweg Airfield. It is interesting to note that between the running of these two Grand Prix meetings not only did Jochen Rindt develop into the fastest driver of his time, but there also took place Austria's elevation to the ranks of the five classic motor racing countries—Britain, Germany, France, Italy and America. Both the foundation and the apex of this pyramid were Jochen Rindt.

To be accurate, its growth began in 1965 at Le Mans.

CHAPTER FOUR

The 21-hour Grand Prix of Le Mans

When fuel companies permit their contracted drivers to race for a competitor, an automatic arrangement comes into effect under which the driver, should he win, may not let his name be used in advertising. This was the situation which faced Jochen before the 1965 twenty-four-hour race at Le Mans. Luigi Chinetti, who won the race three times as a driver, but who never succeeded in doing the same as an entrant, wanted to nominate the BP-contracted Rindt for his Shell-fuelled Ferrari 250 LM.

Druitt's decision was negative, which meant Le Mans was out as far as Jochen was concerned. 'I'll go and see my grandmother in Graz and some friends nearby,' he said. But Chinetti, in his capacity as Ferrari importer for North Africa, exerted some pressure on BP and Druitt gave way. 'Anyway,' he said, 'Rindt couldn't even hope to win a flowerpot with that car.' It certainly did not seem competitive in the face of the Fords and the works Ferraris.

Rindt rang me from the airport on the Thursday before the race and announced he would be co-driving the Ferrari with Masten Gregory. After he had jumped out of still moving sports cars five times between 1957 and 1959, even when it didn't seem absolutely necessary, Gregory became known as 'Catastrophe Masten' or 'Crash me, Gregory', but his driving style was far more aggressive than his character, for Masten is sensitive, only drinks milk and is forever playing chess.

Rindt wins from Graham Hill, Crystal Palace, 1964

Rindt wins from Jimmy Clark, Reims, 1965

Formula Rindt: the start of a Formula 2 race

The 21-hour Grand Prix of Le Mans

Jochen only arrived in time for the last practice period, and started in eleventh place, but at the end of the first hour he was fifth overall and was in amongst the works Fords and Ferraris. After 25 laps, at 17.38, he came in to hand over to Gregory as planned, but the starter motor refused to work and required changing, which cost three laps. Less than 90 minutes later, Masten came in three laps earlier than expected and reported: 'The engine is running on only six of its twelve cylinders; the distributor must have packed up.' Chinetti and team manager Johnny Baus disagreed, believing that Masten must have over-revved and damaged the valves.

Gregory protested in vain, and Rindt was sent out to do a trial lap. He confirmed that only one bank of cylinders was firing. Chinetti proposed to withdraw the car, but Gregory insisted that his theory should at least be investigated. By this stage Rindt had disappeared into the paddock.

It didn't take long to discover a broken condenser, but by the time the distributor had been changed the car had been stationary for 25 minutes.

When the time came for Jochen to take the car out, Masten found him changed and about to depart in his hire-car. 'Where the devil do you think you're going?' asked Masten.

'We've had our race; we can't possibly win,' replied Jochen.

Gregory's low voice had a soothing effect, rather like that of a witch-doctor: 'Are you mad? It is impossible for us to lose as long as we don't have any more problems. Le Mans is a peculiar event. Losing ten laps means nothing.' Jochen accepted but under one condition: 'We drive flat out, to the last lap, until either the car blows up or we win.'

Thus started the 21-hour Grand Prix of Le Mans, even though Masten and Jochen, almost at the end of the field, appeared to have little hope. As the evening turned into darkness, frightening tales reached the North American Racing Team's pit. Jochen was said to have overtaken the

Jochen Rindt

Porsches in the Dunlop curve — a difficult manoeuvre because the cars seem to disappear over the horizon halfway through it. Jackie Stewart reported Jochen to have passed his jet-powered Rover-BRM on two wheels in the Esses. The next time Rindt lapped him, Stewart saw two fingers raised. This process was repeated every five laps, Jochen thinking, quite unmoved, 'Here's that vacuum-cleaner again.'

While Jochen was at the wheel Gregory was told that his co-pilot had gone mad and that he would lose the car sooner or later. When it was Masten's turn, Jochen was informed that his co-pilot was absolutely crazy.

In those days it normally sufficed to change tyres and brake pads just once during the twenty-four hours, but the Gregory/Rindt car ate up six sets of tyres and six sets of pads. The engine was down on power by 300 revs as a result of the distributor change, and this meant that time lost on the straights had to be made up by late braking and ten-tenths cornering.

Thanks to this brutal treatment, the car was showing signs of roughness. The steering transmitted increased vibrations but Jochen was unmoved: 'Either it'll break or it won't.' He even forgot his inhibitions regarding the Huna-dières straight which, at speeds of 180 or more, appeared as narrow as a needle's eye. Earlier he had tried to work out the effects of an accident at that speed, and decided it would be very similar to a plane crash . . .

By this time all the Fords had dropped out, and the works Ferraris were being slowed by brake trouble; in order to improve ventilation the discs had been perforated with air vents, but the rush of cold air at high speed cracked them as they emerged from the corners following heavy braking.

Shortly after dawn, at ten minutes to five, Jochen took Ferrari Number 21 into the lead for the first time. As he had to stop at the pits to refuel shortly afterwards, the lead was admittedly only short-lived. The rest of the morning saw Rindt and Gregory chasing after the Belgian-entered

The 21-hour Grand Prix of Le Mans

Ferrari of industrialist Taf Gosselin and night-club owner Pierre Dumay, both of them spirited amateurs. Ferrari's racing manager Dragoni wanted the drivers to keep their present order, but Chinetti objected and Rindt didn't even listen. He gained five seconds a lap and Gregory four. All this excitement had its effect on the leaders. Gosselin stopped to change a tyre but was told to keep moving. As a result he lost a tread, which tore up the rear bodywork . . . and Rindt/Gregory were undisputedly in the lead.

At 2.30 Gregory arrived for his last refuelling stop: 'Let me drive on, Jochen. I've been trying to win Le Mans for the last ten years, but you still have lots of time.' Jochen agreed. After all, Masten was the older and should be in the car when it crossed the line. A little later there was 'a terrible noise' in every corner. The differential lock was breaking up. The little American, exhausted by the long chase, found a temporary expedient: he disengaged the clutch before each corner, coasted through and then let the clutch in again as gently as possible. His last laps were a full 40 seconds slower than during the earlier chase.

'If he manages to pull through I'll be deliriously happy,' said Jochen into my radio microphone a few minutes before 4 pm. It was only later that he found out about the broken differential, and he realised it was a good thing Masten was at the wheel; he—Jochen—could never have slowed down. Fatigue now hit Masten in an all-enveloping embrace. He couldn't even say anything to Chinetti. And as the mechanics drove the car away to the garage, the differential finally packed up altogether. But they had still won. . . .

Experts now agreed there was only one way to win Le Mans: 'Take it easy during the night and you'll find yourself in front during the morning.' The only trouble is that they were asleep most of the night and thus missed the tremendous chase—the 21-hour Grand Prix.

Jochen and Masten became good friends, even if they continued to disagree for years as to who turned the fastest

Jochen Rindt

lap. Later Gregory moved to Paris and Jochen did likewise. But soon afterwards Gregory was divorced and moved back to New York, returning in 1969 to live near Jochen in Lausanne.

On September 5th 1970, Gregory was once again at Le Mans driving a Chinetti Ferrari, this time a 3-litre for Steve McQueen's new film, when the shock news of Rindt's death arrived from Monza. At Cesenatico, where he scored his first victory, at Crystal Palace and at Le Mans, Jochen's car number was 21; at Monza it was 22.

CHAPTER FIVE

The Cooper Period

All the single-seater racing cars Jochen drove were British: Formula Junior Coopers in 1963 and Formula 1 Coopers from 1965 to 1967; Formula 2 Brabhams from 1964 to 1968, Formula 1 Brabhams in 1968, and after that Formula 1 and Formula 2 Lotuses. John Cooper gave him his first real chance I accompanied Jochen to London early in January 1965 when he signed his three-year contract. It seemed a bit long but he really didn't have much choice. It was a good bargain for Cooper as he was paying Jochen a fairly modest £2,000 annual retainer plus £200 per start, while Jackie Stewart was getting twice as much from BRM. The following year Jackie's contract was doubled again, while Jochen found himself with an insignificant increase. Yet he had the satisfaction of being quicker than Stewart in practice for the South African Grand Prix, the first race of the season. The night before the race, December 31st, meant *Silvester* for the Austrian, Hogmanay for the Scotsman. Both felt somewhat lost among the elite and went to a drive-in movie. 'It was an Oscar prize-winner,' Jackie remembers, 'but Jochen insisted after an hour that we went to bed.' Stewart finished sixth and Rindt retired with faulty electrics, but earlier he had kept up well with his team leader, Bruce McLaren.

Jochen and everybody knew Bruce was planning to build up his own racing team. Somehow the two of them didn't get to know each other terribly well, though Rindt thought it was nice to have Bruce as team mate. Three years earlier,

Jochen Rindt

in Monte Carlo, McLaren had scored Cooper's last Grand Prix victory; it seemed to Rindt that, other than a winning tradition and the memory of John Cooper's pioneering work with rear-engined cars, there was little else left to the team.

A negligent mechanic, fired that same evening, caused Jochen to fail to qualify at Monte Carlo. At Spa he finished eleventh, even though the rev counter dropped out of the dashboard. At Clermont-Ferrand locked brakes caused him to pile into Chris Amon; at Silverstone the engine blew up; at Zandvoort he lost his exhaust system. It was only at this stage of the season that somebody noticed that Jochen's Cooper was fitted with the wrong oil tank! As a person, John Cooper was 'nice and easy' but he seemed to have lost some of his enthusiasm. Admittedly he built an adequate and safe chassis, but he suffered in the engine department with his Climax motors delivering less power than those supplied to Lotus and Brabham; he was no longer a revolutionary.

Shortly afterwards the Cooper Car Company was taken over by the Chipstead Group, headed by Jonathan Sieff, whose family controlled Marks & Spencer. To give the outfit a more competitive edge, Roy Salvadori was appointed team manager; he could be very tough.

Salvadori was considered by many to have been almost as good a driver as Moss, although he never won a Grand Prix. He was deaf in one ear as a result of a crash which was so serious that they gave him the Last Sacrament. When he was driving Coopers in 1959 with Jack Brabham, the latter's car always seemed better prepared, though this was largely because Jack himself spent a lot of time looking after it.

Because of this, Jack and Roy agreed that, if either of them was not satisfied with his car, they would spin a coin and the winner would choose whichever of the cars he wanted. This, however, would not necessarily have helped Roy very much, because Jack always knew which was the better car and Roy did not. In the end they never did actually come to toss for it. At least that's how wealthy businessman Bernie

The Cooper Period

Ecclestone, himself a former racing driver, remembers it. Bernie, who was helping the talented Stuart Lewis-Evans towards his ambition of a championship title in 1958, retired from the scene when his friend was killed at Casablanca in a Vanwall, but began to resume his contacts with Cooper, Brabham and Lotus during 1965. Quite apart from this, he is one of the most personable and likeable people in the high-speed circus.

It was Bernie's theory that Salvadori, in 1965, saw in Jochen a replica of himself ten years earlier. At that time they must have been two of a kind and this led to a tremendous clash of personalities. Neutral observers like Rob Walker noted the non-stop conflict between these two similar personalities.

There you had Salvadori running a team with cars which were not really competitive. It was the last year of the 1½-litre Formula 1 and there just was not time to develop the Cooper-Climax 1500 cc car into a race-winning machine; there was very little Roy could do about it. On the other hand there was Jochen, making desperate efforts to confirm his ability, but having to make do with an inferior machine. As team manager, Roy couldn't really admit that the Cooper wasn't good enough although he did once admit it at Zandvoort with the terse observation: 'Sorry, that car of ours really isn't up to it.'

At the Nürburgring it held together for the first time and Jochen came in fourth behind Clark, Hill and Gurney after a punishing drive in which he was held back for many laps by Bandini. At Monza Jochen finished eighth, and at Watkins Glen sixth, which gave him four championship points for his first Grand Prix season.

In 1966 the 3-litre Formula was introduced and Cooper needed a new engine. His idea was good in principle even if there were commercial implications. The Chipstead Group, increasingly known as the Cooper Group, also owned the Maserati concession for the United Kingdom. It made sense

Jochen Rindt

that if Maserati engines won Grand Prix races, sales of these exotic cars should go up. Additionally John Cooper thought the tie-up might help sell Minis in Italy.

The basically 12-year-old Maserati engines were supplied to Cooper virtually free of charge and were serviced in Modena. The start of the season was promising: Jochen was lying second at Monte Carlo, in spite of having to hold the gear lever in position, but finally he made contact with a slower car, damaging his radiator so severely that he had to retire. In practice at Spa a helicopter returned Jochen to the pits. Stewart asked what ailed him and Jochen replied: 'Nothing, apart from a Maserati engine.' Salvadori, listening to such comments, didn't consider that Jochen was doing much to create a good team relationship.

In the Belgian Grand Prix Rindt found himself on the front row of the grid for the first time and was soon leading the entire field, another personal 'first' in a world championship event. After a chaotic first lap, when all sixteen cars ran into a torrential rainstorm which sent Stewart into hospital, caused serious difficulties to the rest and eliminated no less than eight cars, Jochen battled past the Ferrari of John Surtees and held the lead for 20 of the 28 laps. But four laps from the end a suspected damaged differential cost him his first Grand Prix victory. He had to let Surtees pass.

Salvadori was generous in his congratulations, admitting that the effort was ninety per cent Rindt's, only ten per cent the car's. Even so, an English motoring magazine saw fit to publish its report under the heading of *Surtees supreme at Spa*. One cannot imagine anything much more frustrating as far as Rindt was concerned! Five days later came the divorce, Italian style: Surtees left Ferrari during the Le Mans practice days and joined Rindt in the Cooper-Maserati team.

'Big John' Surtees was serious and totally dedicated to motor racing. It almost seemed that a fire burned within him; he was a 'loner' who tended to isolate himself with his fanaticism. 'It is doubtful whether Surtees, even with his

The Cooper Period

experience, could have been of much help to Jochen,' analysed Bernie Ecclestone, and in any case Jochen didn't want any help. Was this to be another clash of personalities? Bernie was inclined to believe that Salvadori engaged Surtees largely to create driver competition within the team. This move, in fact, resulted in creating two teams within a team: both drivers were allocated their cars, engines and mechanics and were virtually run as two separate entries. Rindt's mechanic, Ronald Dennis, had to admit that Jochen's technical knowledge, in which he didn't have too much faith at first, was growing from race to race.

At Reims, Surtees and Rindt were team mates for the first time. Surtees had to give up after only two laps with an overheated fuel pump; Rindt managed to struggle with his equally afflicted car to finish fourth, in spite of extreme heat. In fact, he lost ten pounds in weight during the two hours of that race. 'Twice I was about to give up. I just wanted to lie in the shade, but something hammered within me: carry on, carry on.'

Surtees also retired at Brands Hatch; Rindt finished fifth and moved up into second place in the world championship table behind Brabham. At Zandvoort a gearbox defect sent him off the road, but he came in third at the Nürburgring and fourth at Monza. 'Now I just live for my car,' he said. 'The Cooper-Maserati really holds the road in wet conditions, but if it's dry we don't have much chance of winning.' At Watkins Glen Rindt hung on behind Jim Clark's Lotus, hoping vainly that Clark's BRM H-16 engine would break, as all the others of this type had done. It didn't break, and thus Rindt had to be content with second place. Finally it was not Rindt but Surtees who obtained the first Cooper-Maserati victory; in Mexico City Surtees won, while Jochen lost a wheel and with it his second place in the Championship.

Thus ended John's interlude with Cooper. He moved over to Honda, and his place was taken by Pedro Rodriguez. Rindt was now not only in third place in the championship,

Jochen Rindt

but collected so many points that he had to drop some of them in accordance with regulations (24 minus 2 equals 22).

In practice for the first race of 1967, the South African Grand Prix, Jochen's engine was staccato-like with its misfire. He asked to try Pedro's car but Roy refused: 'Pedro has made joint second fastest time with Denny Hulme and you've never had your car whipped from under you. Your car will soon be in order.' But there was no improvement on the second day of practice, and Jochen was still not allowed to try out the other car.

The mechanics spent a whole day working on the engine, and Salvadori was sure it was sorted out. Jochen went out for two laps, returned with the engine still spluttering, and settled down to a game of gin rummy with Bernie. Two hours later he had another try-out; the engine still spluttered and he returned to the cards. This went on until 9 pm, with Salvadori's temper steadily deteriorating. In the race Jochen was in front of Pedro until his transmission failed. Pedro, although not particularly well placed initially due to not being able to engage second or third gears in his five-speed gearbox, gradually worked his way up through the field as others fell by the wayside. Finally, local hero John Love ran out of petrol while well in the lead and Pedro won quite unexpectedly. The breach between Rindt and Rodriguez remained right through the season, as neither wanted to make it up.

Rodriguez had few friends in those days among the drivers, but said this didn't bother him as, in contrast to the others, he had his friends outside the race track. He also tended to have a reputation, at least in the early days, for not using his rear-view mirror enough; as his English was poor he couldn't do much in the way of explanations. Today, of course, he is a thoroughly professional driver and probably one of the quickest drivers on the track.

As far as the Maserati engine was concerned, as soon as it started to run reasonably well, the Italians experimented with a view to finding more power. This, of course, put the

The Cooper Period

clock back and the troubles recommenced. What is more, the power output never seemed to be as good in reality as it was on paper. The Maserati-engined Coopers were at an even greater disadvantage when the new Cosworth-Ford-powered Lotus 49s made their first appearance at Zandvoort in the hands of Jim Clark and Graham Hill, the latter recalled to Lotus at Ford's insistence. All of this was a great pity, for the roadholding of the admittedly overweight but strongly constructed Cooper-Maserati was first class, and was frequently praised by Jochen. While Rodriguez collected the odd championship points as a result of his more cautious tactics, Rindt was normally to be found either fighting it out in the leading bunch or watching the race from the pits. He really got the maximum out of the car.

Rindt's only placings in 1967 were fourth at Spa and fourth at Monza, but financially his last year with Cooper was a great improvement as his yearly retainer had shot up to £10,000 as a result of his world championship position the previous year. But money doesn't compensate for disappointments, especially as far as Rindt was concerned.

In preparation for the German Grand Prix a modified engine was tested at Brands Hatch. It was unseasonably cold, and Jochen was suffering from flu. He came in after three laps, but Salvadori sent him out again. He finished the test with a monumental spin at the corner before the pits. Later, at the Nürburgring, he returned to the pits on foot and commented laconically: 'Engine overheated, clutch gone and brakes locked, but otherwise the car is in best possible condition.' At Monza a voice was heard from the darkness at the back of the pit, sounding half like Tom Sawyer and half like Peter Pan: 'Tell me, Roy, why don't our cars look like real racing cars?'

At Watkins Glen Jochen undertook his last long walk back to the pits for Cooper. When his mechanic asked what was the matter with the engine Rindt replied: 'This time it blew up in a really spectacular manner. When I realised it was

Jochen Rindt

about to go, I gave the accelerator pedal an extra kick, which shot the revs up to 12,000, just to make quite sure.' What Jochen didn't realise was that Salvadori was standing behind him, with his sound right ear cocked and not, as usual, the deaf left one! On this dissenting note, Rindt ended his time with Cooper.

CHAPTER SIX

No Car Killer

Jackie Stewart's last season with BRM in 1967 taught him to accept defeat and live with it, providing one was beyond reproach. But Jochen Rindt had to contend with a completely unfounded reputation. 'In the case of most drivers, the reason for their retirement from a race is usually found in their car, but the opposite applies to Rindt. When he drops out it is his own fault; he has burst the engine, overstressed the chassis or overdriven the car in some other way. None of us can really appreciate how much he suffers under this quite undeserved stigma and how hard he tries to cast it off' — so wrote Dieter Stappert, assistant-editor of *Powerslide,* at the time.

It could be that, on one or two occasions in 1967, Jochen might have nursed the Maserati engine along for another couple of laps or so — not that it would have made much difference. It could be that at the time he wasn't able to 'read' his car, the practising or the race itself as well as he did later; that he didn't always digest his lessons as quickly as he might have done.

But if he had really been as hard on his cars as some believed, he would never have finished any of the numerous Formula 2 races in which, too, he always pressed on with ten-tenths effort. The tell-tale needle confirms that, apart from that one episode of the coup de grace at Watkins Glen, he never exceeded the revs set for the Maserati engine. There are other considerations, too. If drivers spent their

Jochen Rindt

entire time watching their rev counter, oil and water temperature gauges, they wouldn't have time to drive as well.

Jochen admitted that he didn't press on quite as hard in 1967 as in 1965 or '66, not to mention 1963 or '64. 'Pressing on regardless doesn't necessarily allow you to go any quicker,' he maintained. 'As I gain in experience, I gradually become an old hand, a veteran as the Americans call it, and this enables me to cut out a certain element of risk.'

Jackie Stewart adds his impression of Jochen's driving style in those earlier days: 'He gets his car sideways to a degree that it requires enormous talent to straighten it out again. Only too often did we imagine he'd really overcooked it . . . but he never did. He was still in command. In fact, this exceptional control over his car is one of his outstanding abilities.'

Significantly neither Stewart nor Jochen, nor any other racing driver, talks about split-second reactions. 'There's not much to choose between us on this point. Reactions are one of the things we don't really recognise. For example, I don't believe I have particularly quick reactions. It's not a question of doing things as quick as lightning; I do things automatically.' And the uncanny ability to spot a gap among fast-moving cars before it actually exists? 'That's not reaction, but intuition,' Stewart fires back.

In 1967, Jackie was still impressed by Jochen's controlled sliding: 'It's quite obvious he likes the four-wheel drift, and he must be disappointed he can't throw the modern Grand Prix car around as much as he might wish. But he is learning rapidly that this is not the quickest way because the fat tyres are bound to slow you down.' However, Jochen considered it was the only way of getting the ponderous Cooper-Maserati up among the leaders, and for 1967 he was probably right.

As for the tales of woe about the poor pre-war drivers who had to make do with those spindly thin tyres, Jochen considered them nonsense. 'The wider these present-day,

No Car Killer

steamroller-like tyres get, the more difficult it becomes to control the car on the straights. Of course, they're much quicker through the corners, but they also reduce that fine difference between sliding and spinning off. Narrow tyres give a far better indication of what is going on; the wider the tyre, the greater the effort needed to drive it.'

In many cases a driver with inferior machinery has to struggle far harder for his ninth or tenth place than those in the lead, yet obtains little acclaim. Inside the Grand Prix circus, however, such efforts are recognised. In his rating for 1967, considered by many to contain the ultimate truth, David Phipps ranked Rindt in second place behind Clark, and above Stewart, Brabham and even the current champion Hulme.

But there was yet another gain to Rindt from this 'Nothing Year', which was so disappointing as far as actual results were concerned. He learned to live with problems and difficulties; to accept them and to reflect about people. In the Cooper team there was much pushing and shoving, which he resented. But there were advantages in experiencing a phase when nothing went right. Character forming, perhaps? It was Salvadori's cynicism and the ruins of the Maserati engines which helped to shape the new character of the 'loner', whom Stewart had spotted at Mallory Park.

It is quite conceivable that Rindt might have given up at the end of 1967 if it hadn't been for the fact that in another sphere, Formula 2, he was able to prove that he could be just as quick as Jim Clark, though Jacky Ickx said in 1970: 'To say that Jochen was the king of Formula 2 was unfair, because it could indicate that there was no place for him on a higher platform.' How right Ickx was.

CHAPTER SEVEN

The Formula 2 Classics

With the exception of Jim Clark and Formula 1 as a whole, no driver ever dominated a form of motor sport as Jochen did in Formula 2. The record shows a victory in 1964 at Crystal Palace, another in 1965 at Reims, two in 1966, at the Nürburgring and Brands Hatch; in 1967 he won at Snetterton, Silverstone, Pau, the Nürburgring, Reims, Rouen, Langenlebarn, Brands Hatch and Haemmenlinna; 1968 at Thruxton, Zolder, Crystal Palace, Hockenheim Ring, Langenlebarn, Enna and Stainz; 1969 at Thruxton, Pau, Zolder and Langenlebarn; and finally in 1970 at Thruxton, Pau, the Nürburgring and Zolder — altogether twenty-nine wins, of which twenty-four were for Team Winkelmann.

The soul of this team, in effect the unofficial Brabham Works Equipe, was that little Welshman Alan Rees; industrialist Roy Winkelmann, living in the USA, was content to give his money and his name — and earned good dividends on both. Chief mechanic was Pete Kerr, a thirty-seven-year-old New Zealander who had come over to England early in 1965 to work on Rindt's car. Jochen frequently claimed that 'in Formula 2 I always feel a hundred per cent safe', and this reflected directly on Kerr's work.

The trio's première was not altogether auspicious: at Oulton Park, Alan broke his transmission during practice. To enable it to be repaired during the night, Jochen used the headlights of Alan's Cortina GT — after this Alan found his windscreen wipers started working when he pressed the

Masten Gregory and Jochen Rindt after their victory at Le Mans, 1965

Jochen (Ferrari number 21) battling with Guichet (Ferrari number 20) during the Le Mans 24-hour Race, 1965

Rindt's Cooper-Maserati during practice for the German Grand Prix, Nürburgring, 1966

The Formula 2 Classics

horn, and eventually he had to abandon the car and take a taxi. The race itself was cancelled owing to snowstorms.

Rindt's first victory for Winkelmann came at Reims in 1965. After an early time-wasting spin he made perfect use of his ability to catch up with Clark and Rees, taking Gardner with him. He nipped by in a sprint finale with the first four cars within inches of each other. At Enna Jochen kicked up stones and dust in front of all and sundry by using the full width of the road, but Alan got his revenge by drawing away to victory. Jochen found the starting money was just enough for a brief holiday in Taormina, where he did his best to tip Alan out of the boat when he found that Alan couldn't swim.

The 1966 season found Jochen obsessed with the idea of getting the better of the hitherto unbeatable Brabham-Hondas, which had 10 bhp more than his Brabham-Cosworth and were driven by Jack and by Denis Hulme. He finally succeeded in doing so in the last race of the series at Brands Hatch. With the nose of his car practically touching Jack's, Jochen played a waiting game. Jack was reckoned to be the most difficult driver to pass. 'If he couldn't stop you any other way, he seemed to throw his car sideways,' was what they said. But Jochen got his chance when they both lapped Chris Lambert. Realising that Lambert could see only him in his mirror, and not Brabham on the inside, Jochen squeezed by and Jack was held up. In spite of all the latter's efforts, and there were few who knew more tricks of the trade than Black Jack, Rindt stayed in front till he passed the chequered flag. 'It was undoubtedly one of the most difficult races I've been in, but I was all the more delighted afterwards,' confessed Jochen later. 'It doesn't matter whether one is driving in a Grand Prix, in Formula 2 or in long-distance events, there comes a point where one feels dead tired. But the more experience I get behind the wheel, the longer I can hold on; now I have little difficulty feeling in top form right through the race.'

Jochen Rindt

Up to 1968 it made some difference to Jochen whether he was running alone or battling wheel to wheel. 'Best of all I like to drive in a gaggle of cars, with at least one or two rivals whom I know I can beat; that doesn't put me under any strain. But if one is driving all on one's own, one is liable to stop concentrating and think of other matters, which can be dangerous.'

It happened to Jochen at Rouen in 1967. He was well in the lead, ahead of Stewart, when he began to daydream and went off the road. He lost the lead but soon began to make up the deficit and Stewart, under pressure, made a nonsense of things and slid off the track. 'A grinning Jochen tore past the pits; it must have been quite something for him to see Stewart on the grass,' recalled Pete Kerr.

Both Stewart and Rindt remember Karlskoga 1967 as being a particularly close fight throughout. Near the end Jochen lost all his water, and on the last lap the cylinder block cracked. Helmut Marko, driving a Formula Vee car at the time, remembers how Jochen's face suddenly fell when he saw the jubilant reception Stewart received, while no-one seemed to remember his own fantastic drive.

Jochen remembers the hectic dash from the Canadian Grand Prix that year to the Formula 2 race at Brands Hatch the next day. 'We had to fly through the night with no time to spare; I won at Brands, but this sort of slave-driving really isn't very clever.' Not quite as exhausting was the journey from the British Grand Prix to Langenlebarn. Clark emerged at around midnight from Hill's plane, still wearing his driving shoes, and Jochen arrived shortly afterwards with Jack Brabham — only to spend two hours on the telephone trying to get a taxi. He finally managed a few hours' sleep just before the race in the local army barracks . . . and won.

With his nine outright victories and four second places in fifteen events, Jochen really turned the 1967 Formula 2 into Formula Rindt. If the world championship scoring had applied he would have gained 107 points; no-one else would

The Formula 2 Classics

have scored more than 50. He won both the British and French Formula 2 championships hands down, competing against people like Clark, Stewart and Hill. Sometimes he just ran away from them all. If people considered Clark worth an extra second per lap in Formula 1, then the same applied to Rindt in Formula 2.

'Formula 2 was set up in 1964 in order to enable drivers as well as organisers not engaged in Formula 1 to get used to the pace of big time racing. Somehow all that changed in 1967, perhaps thanks to my domination,' according to Jochen's analysis, 'because some are afraid they will lose both cash and fame if they can't keep in front of the up and coming drivers. That is why a number of people retired quietly. In practice therefore it was only Jimmy, Jackie and sometimes Graham who battled it out in front with me, although in 1968 the Matras will be the team to beat.'

For 1968 the Winkelmann team was sponsored by BP-Austria. In April Jochen was able to cable back from Thruxton: 'First race, first win for you. If that isn't service . . .' But the Limburg Grand Prix early in May was even better. Jochen considered it his best race, at least till Monte Carlo 1970.

In practice he was a tenth of a second quicker than Amon's Ferrari, and three-tenths quicker than Beltoise's Matra and Redman's Lola. He won the first heat with ease, heading Amon by 9.5 seconds and Irwin by over 30, and this gave him pole position for the second heat as well.

But just as Jochen let in his clutch Redman, perhaps a little over-keen, catapulted into him. Jochen spun the length of the grid; incredibly he hit no-one and no-one crashed into him. The thick black tyre marks pointed directly at the pit where Nina watched the race with Debbie, Alan's fiancée, and the shock nearly made her fall off the tyre on which she was perched.

The Brabham finished up with its nose pointing in the wrong direction, but Jochen flung the car round and chased

Jochen Rindt

after the pack. Pete Kerr rushed to Nina's assistance and pressed a stop-watch into her hand to keep her busy. Jochen soon caught up; tenth by the hairpin, seventh at the end of the first lap and sixth on the third. Then he forced his way past Irwin and Pescarolo to tackle the leading Ferraris of Ickx and Amon. Stirling Moss told me what he said on this occasion, speaking of Rindt: 'There are nowadays a number of outstanding drivers, but very few like Jochen who, when the odds are against him, fights like a tiger.'

Of course, Jochen couldn't 'tiger' in every race. But this important quality of being able to utilise his natural talent to the full was never shown more impressively than at Zolder; never before had he demonstrated his capacity to pull the stops out when circumstances demanded it. He overtook in places where it looked impossible; he turned in lap times which seemed highly improbable. He broke his own lap record, set up during the first heat, by no less than nine-tenths of a second. There was consternation in the Ferrari pit. Ickx was shown a signal which indicated that he should allow Amon to pass him; if Amon won the heat he would be the outright winner, having finished second in the first heat; if Ickx stayed in front there was a chance that Rindt would beat both Ferraris. But Ickx stayed in front.

Jochen tried to outbrake Amon at the hairpin on the last lap, but selected second gear instead of first and didn't make it. So Ickx won by 3.1 seconds from Amon, with Rindt another 1.8 seconds behind. This put him first equal on points, but he was declared the winner because of his better overall time.

'Am I the winner? Did I win?' spluttered Jochen before his car had even quite stopped. 'Do you realise you almost knocked down half the people in the pits?' Pete Kerr asked. Jochen looked amazed. Having concentrated one hundred per cent on winning the race, he had forgotten all about that first lap incident: typical Jochen.

Later, in 1969 and 1970, when things became a little bit dull

The Formula 2 Classics

for him, Jochen would remember Zolder and wish for another race like it so as to force him into another ten-tenths effort. He liked to be reminded that he could win even if things went wrong.

Rindt quickly forgot unlucky incidents. During practice in Pau he buckled the Brabham's rear-end. The next day Rees became involved in someone else's shunt. 'Alan, you road-hog,' reprimanded Jochen; he had already forgotten that much the same had happened to him the previous day. On another occasion Jochen lost it in a big way at Pau near the Casino, when leading Stewart and Hill. 'My God, this is going to be a major shunt,' thought Stewart, braking hard. 'Jochen slid sideways right down the track and ploughed into the rose gardens, with flowers flying everywhere – but when he got back on the road, he was even further ahead, because we had been slowing down!' In 1968 both Rindt and Stewart switched to Dunlop in Formula 2. 'We did most of our testing with Winkelmann. Rees saw to that; Jochen just set up his car accordingly,' recalls Iain Mills of Dunlop. 'And Jochen always wanted tyres an inch wider than Stewart as well as higher pressures.'

Normally it is largely a question of luck who wins Formula 2 slipstream races, like the ones at Hockenheim before they built the chicane. But this was not the case when Jochen won. Even if he was lying as far back as ninth on the penultimate lap, he still seemed to control the actions of the other drivers. To many Formula 2 drivers, the sight of Jochen in their rear view mirrors meant a much-feared slipstream battle. Rindt didn't like these battles. 'They are damned dangerous, with perhaps twenty drivers striving like idiots for one point and no-one wanting to brake first.' At Hockenheim, after one of Rindt's successes, Kerr asked him: 'What was your oil pressure?' Jochen mumbled something about 80 pounds. Kerr seemed satisfied and Jochen grinned: 'A good guess, what?'

When driving in Formula 2 Jochen gave full credit to the

car and to his mechanics; he didn't seem to appreciate that his skill at the wheel had played the major part. Alan Rees decided to retire after the Argentine Temporada. When they arrived over there he and Jochen found their Cosworth engines down on power in comparison with the Ferraris of de Adamich and Brambilla, 'and our only chance of winning was lost by an odd turn of events'.

Because it was so hot they decided to skip the first day of practice and take a riding trip into the Andes. Alan was with Debbie, Jochen with Nina. When they returned that night a sandstorm was raging, engulfing the whole of the track. The next day's practice was accordingly cancelled. For the first and only time, both Winkelmann Brabhams were on the last row of the grid. 'On the very first corner Rindt outbraked six cars,' recalls Rees, 'and that was the last I saw of him.' But the Temporada of 1968 was significant for another reason: it saw the beginning of what was to become a virtually inseparable foursome around the Grand Prix race tracks: Piers and Sally Courage, Jochen and Nina Rindt.

CHAPTER EIGHT

Nina

Both Nina and Sally worked as photographic models on a part-time basis. Both their fathers were well-known racing drivers: Nina's father, Kurt Lincoln from Finland, drove in Formula 2, Formula Junior and sports cars during the fifties and the early sixties; Sally's father, the very English Lord Howe, was active during the old Brooklands days. Both men survived their sport and both girls met their future husbands at the race track as they worked, oily and dirty, on their cars. Sally met Piers in England, and Nina met Jochen in Budapest in 1963.

'He looks amusing,' Nina thought, but Jochen hardly noticed her. She was accompanied by her brother Lasse, now twenty-eight. Their father stopped him becoming a racing driver after a serious traffic accident; instead he turned to tennis, played in the Wimbledon Junior Tournament and is still a member of the Finnish Davis Cup team. Besides this, Nina's mother belongs to the Finnish Bridge Team.

Nina remembers standing at the foot of a steep ski slope the following winter at Zürs when some character shot down at fantastic speed and swerved to a spectacular halt in front of her. She told her father that this was the racing driver they had met last summer: 'You know, the one with a funny nose.' Her father disagreed: 'Impossible, racing drivers don't ski.' Nina's family—half Swedish, half Russian (her grandfather still lives in Moscow today)—ran into Jochen at

Jochen Rindt

teatime. Kurt Lincoln introduced Nina and Lasse. Jochen was surprised he had children, yet Nina was twenty. Jochen suggested they all meet that evening in the 'Kuhbar'.

To Nina's disappointment he only talked to his friends, and when he finally got around to dancing with her, well after midnight, it was only because everybody told him to. 'We stayed on another ten days but Jochen only kept me company on the ski slopes.'

Soon after Nina moved to Brussels where she studied haute couture. Jochen often visited her on his way to England. 'We became engaged for about six months but it didn't quite work out because of my driving and her career.' Nina recalls it this way: 'Jochen was quite impossible at twenty-two. He tried to impress me with his money and his racing, but I made it clear I wasn't interested in either.'

She started to work in a fashion house, but Jochen took her away to Albi and Pau and that was the end of that particular job. In 1964 she had just decided to join Pan American as an air-hostess and was on the point of leaving for London when Jochen turned up: 'Are you joking? You want to become an airborne waitress?'

Oddly enough, many future racing wives started off with quite different plans for the future. Bette Hill, for example, became engaged to a lieutenant in the Canadian Marines and had booked her ship's passage when Graham whisked her away at the last moment. Helen McGregor of Scotland was supposed to follow her parents' wish and marry a dreamy concert pianist before a certain Jackie Stewart made his appearance.

'Whatever I decided to do, Jochen stopped me before I started,' Nina complained. 'He wanted me all for himself. So I turned back to photographic modelling because it was less inconvenient.' Nina posed for *Vogue, Life, Look, Mademoiselle, Elle* and every Finnish magazine there is. She was paid $60 an hour or $360 per day.

For two years total silence reigned between Nina and

Nina

Jochen. She didn't reply to any of his letters and even returned his engagement ring. She received it back by return of post, with just three words: *Keep it. Jochen.*

Her family continued to spend their Christmas holidays in Zürs and so did Jochen, but he always left the day before the Lincolns arrived. However, in 1966 he telephoned her from the airport: 'I'm on the way to South Africa but I'd like to talk to your father about a Formula Vee race at Keimola.' Nina told him she would be in New York in January. 'Me too,' replied Jochen, 'because I'm driving at Daytona. Maybe we'll meet.'

And so it came to pass. Nina realised that Jochen had changed completely. 'Now that he's got somewhere in motor racing, he can think about building up himself.' New York, the Bahamas, then Sebring, Daytona, Florida: during the evening of the 12-hour race, Jochen's partner Gerhard Mitter took over. Suddenly he entered the caravan—where Jochen was whiling away the time with Nina—looking downcast: 'The engine is finished, I am sorry. Are you upset?' Jochen jumped up: 'No, not today.'

The wedding date was fixed, and Nina telephoned her mother to ask her to make all the necessary preparations. 'But who?' was the puzzled reply. 'Her parents are pleased it's me, in spite of my occupation,' Jochen said. 'After all, the racing atmosphere is nothing new in that family.' The wedding was to take place in Helsinki's oldest church on March 5th 1967, as that was Rindt's last race-free weekend.

Jochen asked Lemmy Hofer to make him a morning suit at minimum notice, as he had never had one and hadn't ever thought he would need one. The honeymoon was spent in Zürs, but lasted only four days because Jochen was entered for the Race of the Champions at Brands Hatch. Jochen was not pleased to have to break off his honeymoon because of a race in 'that damned Cooper', as he put it to Masten Gregory in the pits. Nina squatted on a pile of tyres, frozen stiff, and hadn't even got a stop-watch.

Jochen Rindt

'I don't intend to make a racing driver's wife out of her but she'll have to accompany me to a few races,' reflected Jochen. But before long Nina recognised she must decide whether to work or to travel with her husband. She decided for Jochen and thus for motor racing. But neither of them knew where they should live: London, or Paris, or Switzerland? They chose Paris because Nina could more easily find work in the fashionable metropolis. Nina tramped from one estate agent to another and looked at more than fifty flats before she found the right one; it was Number 137, Rue de la Tour in the elegant XVIe Arrondissement. 'But before we could move in Indianapolis intervened, and as Jochen wanted me to go along we were left with a home without furniture.'

Jochen went to Indy with mixed feelings. To the Americans, because of its startlingly high prize money, its speeds and its accident-proneness, it signifies at one and the same time a gold mine, a cathedral and a sacrificial altar. He tried to imagine what would happen if the 'gas pedal' stuck wide open, in one of those high-speed corners.

The reaction of most racing drivers would be to try, in spite of everything, to take that corner—quite a job when it will allow you to get through at only 160 mph, and you are doing over 200. 'I would try to spin the car and, with luck, try to hit the wall at the most acute angle possible.' Of course, to aim a car at the wall under any circumstances would require considerable courage as well as a cool head!

Inevitably, Jochen was faced with just that problem: the accelerator jammed. He steered the spinning Eagle into the retaining wall, contacted it at a good angle and slid along it. Both his right-hand wheels were torn off and the car rode up, freeing the left rear wheel and causing the engine revs to exceed 12,000. It exploded in an enormous fireball, enveloping the whole area in black smoke, according to shocked eye-witness Leo Mehl, Goodyear's racing manager.

Jochen was afraid of breaking every bone in his body if

Nina

he jumped out so he steered the raging inferno of a car as long as possible, released his safety harness and abandoned ship when the speed had come down to reasonable limits. Fire tenders were on the scene within four seconds of the conflagration having started.

Indy rules insist that any driver who has been in collision with another car or with the wall must be taken to hospital immediately for a thorough check-up. Typically, Jochen climbed into the cab of the ambulance, after having shut the loading door at the back, calmly settled down and offered the driver a cigarette! He even opened the main gate for him. The doctors were astounded to find his pulse rate up by only two beats; it was four days before Jochen realised just how dangerous a situation he had survived. Days later sketches illustrating the accident were still displayed in the press office with the addendum *Rindt OK* repeated several times over — they couldn't believe it either. 'A headache and a bit of a fright, that's all,' Jochen said when I arrived.

Leo Mehl found another car for Jochen, but Jackie Stewart was quicker and bumped Rindt from the list of 33 qualifiers. Jochen tried another Eagle and put it to good use; he qualified for the last row of the grid between American driver Al Miller, of Red Indian origin, and Graham Hill.

The evening before the 500, I found myself with Jochen, Nina and Denny Hulme in a local steak house. Jochen was depressed. 'Every European driver here feels as if he's on the way to his funeral. I'm only here for the money. But if you haven't a chance of winning, the entire dangerous business is senseless. Indy frightens me. The Americans don't look in their mirrors, the officials think they know it all and the regulations are just childish; anyway, it's utterly boring to have to practise for thirty days for just one three-hour race, and to get nowhere during those thirty days.'

Before the start Jochen asked me what was meant by 'Memorial Day'. I told him it's an American All Souls' Day,

Jochen Rindt

perhaps more like Armistice Day. Jochen's reply was soft and cynical: 'What an omen for the race.'

I tried in vain to smuggle Nina into the pits. Women are simply not allowed in at Indy. After 121 laps Jochen was forced to retire with engine trouble. He signed a few autographs for the Eagle mechanics, thanked them, and flew back to Paris with Nina, richer by $10,571, to buy some antique furniture.

In Paris, Jochen and Nina met Jim Clark for lunch practically every day. Jim was staying with racing journalist Jabby Crombac in St. Germain; Jochen and Jimmy became good friends. Jochen had problems because Nina's friends were almost exclusively French-speaking, and he also got terribly lost in the Paris traffic. 'Although we lived in Paris for over a year, I always needed a navigator when I went back there. As the telephone system was impossible and there was never any parking space at the airport, Nina and I decided in 1968 to move to Switzerland.' They settled for the Lake Geneva area, rather than the more remote Lugano district where Jochen had had a flat since 1965.

Jochen was shocked at the prices: 'One millionairess demanded half a million dollars for an old castle complete with ghosts.' Stewart helped him out by finding a chalet to rent near his home at Begnins. But shortly before the 1970 Spanish Grand Prix their temporary abode was sold, so they had to move on. A clever lawyer, Dr Pfyffer, found a way out: he had the keys of ex-heavyweight boxing champion Ingemar Johansson's Le Muids; empty, because he travels all the year with his all-in wrestlers.

Johansson's furniture was consigned to the basement, which was to please him later on, as he always intended to refurnish. The timber chalet, with its sauna and swimming pool, and with a tree trunk dividing the living room, was good value—as a temporary expedient—at £150 per month.

Earlier Jochen had purchased some land from Joakim Bonnier and had designed a house to go on it; he had even

Nina

made a cardboard model. Nina was pleased that her taste and Jochen's coincided, although Jochen warned that only God and the architect knew when the house would be ready. For Rindt, citizen of Europe, this was to be the final residence — for Nina, himself and Natascha.

Originally Jochen and Nina wanted a boy first, 'but it really makes little difference because with a boy the difficulties come early on while with a girl they start later.' Natascha was born three days after the German Grand Prix on August 7th 1968; her second Christian name was Jonin, the combination of her parents' first names. Proud father though he was, it was not the child which barred him from further success but the Repco engine, for he was now with the Brabham team.

CHAPTER NINE

'Black Jack'

'I can change teams easier than you can,' Jochen used to say to Salvadori in 1967. For 1968 he had offers from every racing stable except Lotus. But he was attracted by the idea of driving for a private entrant; not surprising when one compares the goings-on in the Cooper team with his favourable experiences in Formula 2.

Winkelmann, Firestone and BP were prepared to sponsor such a project, expensive though it would be. Jochen was thinking in terms of a Brabham chassis; if he couldn't get one he would ask Robin Herd to design a car. Robin, only two years older than Jochen, was already considered a technical whizz-kid; a fabulous degree at Oxford; from 1961 to 1965 in a leading role with the Concorde project; since then behind the McLaren team.

Robin's design for Jochen was ready on the drawing board when the let-down came: Firestone changed their racing policy and BP retired altogether. McLaren decided to make a Ford-engined Formula 1 car and took over Robin's design. This became the M7, which took Hulme and McLaren to third and fifth places in the 1968 world championship table.

'In 1968 Jochen's private Formula 1 team would hardly have been feasible, although it could have been possible later,' according to Jack Brabham. At Monza, Jack and Jochen discussed the possibilities of some sort of partnership. Jack considered Jochen to be the fastest driver available. 'With just a little additional experience, he is bound

'Black Jack'

to be world champion sooner or later. And when that time comes, I'd like him to be driving one of my cars.'

Jochen said 'no' to Ferrari and Matra. He got his mechanic, Ron Dennis, to change from Cooper to Brabham, and Ron soon became of great help to Jack and Ron Tauranac in preparing the new BT-26 chassis. There was one snag; Jochen obviously wasn't going to get rich at Brabham's. 'Naturally, I'd like to make as much as possible, but the main objective is to win,' Jochen explained. And Brabham believed he could give Rindt the one thing worth more than money: the world championship. After all, his cars had twice won the supreme title; in 1966 with Jack driving and in 1967 with Denny Hulme at the wheel.

When Brabham arrived in England in 1955, shy and a little lost, he found people were prepared to respect him about as much as the Australians respected those who emigrated to Australia to look for gold. At any rate, that's how Bernie Ecclestone saw the arrival of the Australian dirt-track champion. Later his fellow-countryman Ron Tauranac followed; Team Brabham was complete.

Their recipe for success lay not in revolutionary or sensational designs, but in soundly improving the recipe from the previous year. Every single component was checked, proven and tested. Anything which might not be strong enough was changed or reinforced. Their formula for success was simple: the car must be safe, fast and easy to maintain. There are only two weeks' interval between Grands Prix, and transit time reduces this still further. There is no time for any magic.

Brabham cars are adaptable; they suited Jochen's driving style. Tauranac believes his chassis make things easier for the drivers; make them work less hard.

Jochen was to get the best prepared car; Jack would always stand down for him, just as he had done for Dan Gurney. Jochen had tremendous respect for Jack. He admired his attitude to motor racing; dedicated professionalism, yet without unnecessary dramatics. This was how Jochen wanted to be. He used Brabham as his yardstick; he wanted to be like him. He put his trust in him totally, and in return Jack took him under his wing. 'Driving for Jack is reassuring: he drives the same car and thus makes sure it is safe, in contrast to other car constructors who don't have to put their theories to the test.'

In South Africa, the opening Grand Prix of the season, Rindt was placed third—and first non-Ford-engined driver —behind the Lotuses of Clark and Hill. It was to be Jimmy's last Grand Prix.

I often recall a flight from Madrid to Paris when Alan Rees confided to Jochen: 'There are three drivers today with such ability that nothing should happen to them; they can think ahead of danger.' He meant Jimmy, Dan Gurney and Jochen. 'I would have added Jackie Stewart to that list,' said Jochen.

Pit signal: Jochen leads a Grand Prix for the first time; the Cooper-Maserati at Spa, 1966

Jochen driving the Brabham, Nürburgring, 1968

The Rindt Lotus spins into the banking at Indianapolis, 1969

CHAPTER TEN

'The Line between Success and Disaster is Very Thin'

The drizzle at the Hockenheim circuit appeared just as depressing as two months earlier at Longford, the last race of the Tasman series, when Jim Clark and Chris Amon had to work hard to keep their cars on the slippery track. They were lined up next to each other on the third row of the grid. 'This is going to be a second Longford,' said Jimmy. Chris, no more cheerful, replied: 'That's for bloody sure.' A few minutes later Clark was dead.

The news reached Jochen in the pits at Brands Hatch during the BOAC 500 prototype race and it shattered him. 'Jimmy was the one I was with most frequently, and we were pretty close friends, as much as this is possible in motor racing.'

Perhaps for the first time Jochen tried to analyse seriously the dangers which motor racing involved; he knew that the fate which overtook Clark could next be his.

Jochen didn't think there was any doubt about the future of the Lotus team; but in Jimmy, Colin Chapman had lost his partner and friend. They grew together into Grand Prix racing and Colin said, 'He was the best friend I ever had or ever will have. My very best friend.'

I knew that whenever a Ferrari driver was killed, his photograph disappeared from Ferrari's desk and found a place in the room next door. It made me wonder how the

Jochen Rindt

Englishman would react. Over two years later, when I sat with Chapman in the overseas lounge of the Earls Court Motor Show and we found time to review the human as well as the technical aspects of the Hockenheim tragedy, he tended to put the blame on the whole system.

'This entire motor racing business is a question of feelings of triumph one moment and of utter despair the next. One has to learn therefore to control one's feelings; if one doesn't, one just goes mad. But that doesn't mean one has no feelings.

'One simply has to be without pity; the line between success and disaster is very, very thin — the difference between the driver who walks away after an accident and the one who dies is just as thin. I would say that for each fatal accident there are ninety-nine where the driver escapes. You have to look at motor racing from this point of view.'

On the question of blame, Chapman has very definite views: 'When someone is killed in one of my cars, then I accept responsibility, but not blame. We are all to blame, the whole of the Grand Prix circus; we must accept equal blame. Whether the accident had any direct connection with one of my cars or not, is not the point. Several young drivers whom I greatly admired have died, and each time it has made me question the sanity of motor racing. But there are so many ways of getting killed; nowadays it even happens to politicians. It is surely admirable that there are still individuals today who do something because they like doing it, even though they realise just what the risks are. Life would be terribly colourless without risk. Racing drivers offer to millions of the public pleasure, entertainment, excitement and inspiration; death is part of this. Their life may be dangerous but it's also full of glory. The driver may be hurt but he receives his share of fame and adulation. You only get what you pay for. You can't have it both ways.

'Unfortunately things do go wrong, not for reasons of negligence, but because of ignorance or human fallibility, both of which are virtually impossible to eliminate.'

'The Line between Success and Disaster is Very Thin'

And Chapman agreed one can learn from accidents, and claimed that perhaps Jim Clark's death has saved the lives of all those drivers who hit the safety rails at the Hockenheim circuit after April 7th 1968, for before that date there weren't any.

What was the cause of the Clark accident? Chapman's theory is the result of the investigation of aircrash experts from Farnborough: 'The right rear tyre was cut, not as the result of its collision with a tree, but apparently due to a slow puncture.'

In Chapman's view, the sequence of events at Hockenheim was as follows: Clark drove over a stone, nail or similar object and that right rear tyre was damaged. The air escaped slowly and lowered the pressure. An eye witness confirmed that in the last left-hand bend Clark almost lost control of the Lotus, but was able to correct instantly. He presumably thought his tyres didn't suit the wet track; it didn't occur to him that one of them was damaged, nor did he feel anything in the next two right-hand corners because the weight of the car was transferred to the wheels on the left. And even the straight he entered next curved gently to the right. By this time, according to Chapman's theory, the pressure in the damaged tyre would have dropped to eight or ten pounds. Even this pressure would keep the tyre on its rim up to 120 or 130 mph—this was established during subsequent tests—but 1600 cc Formula 2 cars go considerably faster than this on the long curving right-hander at Hockenheim.

'Rapid decompression, equivalent to an explosion, follows and the tyre is torn from the rim,' explained Chapman. 'The car is thrown completely out of balance and cannot possibly be controlled.'

Chapman finalised this theory soon after the accident, but it was not until eighteen months later, during the 1969 US Grand Prix at Watkins Glen, when Graham Hill had the misfortune to suffer a similar accident and suffered serious

Jochen Rindt

injury in the process, that any support for the theory was forthcoming.

Graham slid wide on a patch of oil, ran over some earth and stones, pushed the Lotus back on to the track and continued without realising that he had suffered damage to his left rear tyre. The mechanics and most of the 30,000 spectators near the pits noticed the deflating tyre, but not Hill. When he reached the critical speed—in this case about 160 mph—a serious accident became inevitable. 'At once I saw a parallel to Clark's accident,' says Chapman, 'because everything happened the same way. But this time we learned from it, as we always try to learn: we installed safety bolts in the wheel rims in order to retain even a deflating tyre.'

Jochen Rindt had this to tell me with regard to the tyre situation at the end of 1969: 'The modern racing tyre is a work of art, backed by the collective know-how of the tyre manufacturer. Highly qualified technicians develop the most advanced product possible. But these tubeless tyres are designed for the track. If you have the misfortune to leave the track, your fate is in the lap of the gods.'

Formula 1 teams and tyre manufacturers are closely interdependent; close collaboration is to the advantage of both and revolves around three considerations: development, success and money. Even those who doubt the value of motor racing cannot deny the tremendous progress which has taken place in tyre design and safety.

'These race tyres give the engineers a mass of data and information which is gradually fed into the production lines,' Jochen said. 'Whether it is a question of tread pattern or rain tyres, the compound or anything else, the Grand Prix tyres of the mid-fifties wouldn't be good enough today even for everyday cars driven in a reasonably sporting manner.' If you include development costs, the price of a single racing tyre can be as high as £70; as both Firestone and Goodyear realised it was not only better but certainly much cheaper

'The Line between Success and Disaster is Very Thin'

to manufacture race tyres in Europe, they transferred their production to England. This meant Jochen could be of considerable help to Goodyear racing manager Leo Mehl in his Wolverhampton headquarters.

One by-product of this collaboration is the system of bonus payments whereby tyre manufacturers pay Grand Prix winners something in the region of £2,000; second place is worth £1,000; and third £650. Firestone's racing budget for 1968 amounted to about £3,500,000. They and other tyre firms paid their Formula 1 teams on a yearly contract basis anything up to £100,000, and this financial support was absolutely vital to the teams—particularly as the fuel companies, which were so generous in the days of the cheaper 1.5-litre formula, had become much more budget conscious. But even the tyre companies don't meet the full bill, although Dunlop was reckoned in 1968 to have financed about ninety per cent of Jackie Stewart's and the Tyrrell team's expenses; while Goodyear habitually paid more to Brabham than Firestone did to Lotus.

Luckily this scaling down of support resulted in other sponsors entering this field, most of them quite unconnected with motor racing. Thus Lotus concluded an agreement with Gold Leaf cigarettes, BRM with Yardley and McLaren with Reynolds Aluminium.

In addition some tyre companies have exclusive contracts with certain top drivers; for example Mario Andretti received half a million dollars from Firestone for a four-year contract. For the elite Grand Prix drivers the fee paid by tyre firms has been as high as $50,000 per annum; in most cases this has also included Indianapolis.

CHAPTER ELEVEN

Under Brabham's Wing

To fill the gap in Team Lotus, Colin Chapman approached Piers Courage, then driving for Parnell-BRM, but Piers preferred to be a big fish in a little pond rather than the other way round. He was the third driver to turn down an offer from Chapman; Surtees did so in 1961 when he found out Chapman already had certain commitments with regard to Innes Ireland; and Stewart refused in 1967 'because I had the feeling that Colin would try to play Jimmy and me against each other'.

The Indianapolis Lotus—which Clark would have driven, which Stewart was unable to drive because of his broken wrist and which Chris Amon had declined to drive—was handed to Mike Spence, who was killed in practice on May 7th 1968, exactly a month after Jim Clark. Spence died when one of his front wheels hit him after the car was in collision with the wall.

But luck turned for Chapman in the Spanish Grand Prix, which was won by Hill. Neither of the Brabham drivers finished; in fact they almost missed the start because they were in the pits drinking tea. In the ensuing rush somebody forgot to close Jochen's petrol cap and the car spilled fuel all over the place during the warming-up lap. This delayed him for ten seconds at the start, and while he was trying to catch up the Repco engine overheated.

At Monte Carlo Bernie, Salvadori and Rindt shared the boat *Unica II* which they had rented for 15,000 francs,

Under Brabham's Wing

'cheaper than the Hotel de Paris'. Roy Salvadori unselfishly lowered himself to cook for Jochen, even though Jochen teased him—'As always the most charming thing about you is your wife.'

'I'll have to slow Jochen down somehow so he doesn't tear away from the grid like he did last year, when he would have won by two laps if he had lasted all the way,' Bernie said before the race. Jochen was in the third row behind Hill and the sensation of practice, Johnny Servoz-Gavin. 'Don't worry, the Matra won't last eighty laps,' Bernie said. 'Correction, the Matra might last, but Johnny won't last,' Jochen replied. As always before races run in great heat, which he never liked, Jochen stuffed asbestos soles into his shoes.

Servoz-Gavin went out as expected after leading for four laps, but he had touched the chicane *'très, très peu'* already in the opening lap. This left Jochen fourth behind Hill, Siffert and Surtees, and on the ninth lap he tried to get past the Honda on the descent to the Mirabeau Hotel. Surtees was having difficulty changing gear and Rindt was determined to pass, but the manoeuvre finished in the guardrails with the Brabham minus one wheel. Shortly afterwards Surtees stopped at the pits. 'Suddenly I saw a shadow; it must have been Jochen!' he explained.

Nina closed her lap chart and ran up the hill to the Casino to meet Jochen walking back to the pits. Later, down by the port, he saw Jack Brabham, holding a bolt in his hand. 'You too?' asked Jochen. Jack just grinned and carried on.

'It was all my fault,' Jochen said, 'and I wouldn't blame anyone. Surtees drove quite correctly—though I couldn't be that relentless.' 'All ex-motor cyclists are like that,' Salvadori consoled him.

On the yacht the discussion continued all night. A Brabham story circulated. 'The only time I found myself in real danger was at Indianapolis in 1964. After the fatal crashes of Sachs and MacDonald we all ran, braking hard, into the wall of fire which resulted. I decided to try to skirt the right-hand edge of the inferno, changed my mind for no particular reason at the last moment, and steered to the left. This saved my life because the right-hand path was completely blocked by burning wrecks. But I'd still like to drive again at Indy.'

Jochen's new chassis was ready in time for the Belgian Grand Prix. Jack wanted to try out an idea which appealed to him particularly because of his flying experience: if wings give lift to aircraft by means of the airstream which passes beneath the aerofoil, then the opposite could be made to apply to racing cars, using an aerofoil section of reverse shape to give a down pressure effect. This in turn would enable the car to increase its speed through corners. The first appearance of a 'wing' in public had been when one was fitted experimentally to his car by Jim Clark during the Tasman Series of 1968.

Enough has been written about the 'wing menace', an epidemic which grew worse from race to race. It is a fact that no standards were laid down by the international motor sports bodies until 1969. Jochen always distrusted them intensely, but no-one could afford to do without them. As Ken Tyrrell, Stewart's team manager, put it: 'These wings will save at least one or two seconds per lap, and no-one can give that away.'

There is an old truism that if you want to find something out badly enough, you will do so, and this certainly applies to the extremely competitive situation in Formula 1 racing. Perhaps Ferrari got the idea from Brabham; anyway, Ickx and Amon appeared with their 'aeronautical' cars at Spa. In fact, because the Brabham transporter was delayed and then somewhat slow in disgorging its load, Ferrari were given the credit of being first in this field.

During the practice both Jack and Jochen had fuel feed problems. One likely cause was the earlier departure from the team of three fuel injection experts. Jack flew back to

Under Brabham's Wing

England to obtain new engines and this became typical of the 1968 season: Brabham had to spend so much time flying in new power units that he scarcely had time to practise. On Saturday a typical Spa downpour set in; depressed, Stewart discussed with Jochen ways and means of reducing the resultant dangers on this ultra-fast but twisting course, set in the midst of the Ardennes: 'It is no longer a question of who'll win but of who will drive and who will refuse.' When I reminded Jochen of his epic struggle in the rain in 1966 he just dismissed it by saying: 'Yes, but then I was young and foolhardy.' Into this already depressing atmosphere dropped the shock news that Ludovico Scarfiotti had been killed at Rossfeld. According to Ferrari's former racing manager, Franco Lini, 'Dodo' had been under great strain for some time. 'So they seem to have pushed him too hard, or perhaps he was pushing himself too relentlessly,' said Jochen to me. 'And that's the good thing about the Brabham team: nobody expects me to go flat out. We know our turn will come to start winning.'

Race day dawned fine and dry and Rindt and Brabham were on the back row, but by the end of the first lap Rindt was ninth. A lap later and he stopped at the pits covered in oil. He was furious: 'Siffert, of course, they always overfill his oil tank.'

Two laps in arrears Jochen rejoined the fray but before long both he and Brabham had to give up with valve trouble. Bruce McLaren won his first Grand Prix for four years after Stewart, driving a fantastic race in spite of his wrist injury, ran out of fuel on the last lap. Jochen recalled that while still driving he was well ahead of McLaren. . . .

'But my car is really running beautifully, and if only the engine lasts it should do well at Zandvoort.' As always Jochen's car received priority attention when it came to race preparation. 'At first Jochen had little interest in this side of things, but he learned fantastically quickly,' insisted his mechanic, Ron Dennis.

Jochen Rindt

In fact Jochen developed capabilities quite unsuspected earlier on. He could now tell Jack exactly what went wrong with the car and Jack, with his practical knowledge, could then put it right. Jochen liked the car with the suspension set up as tautly as possible, because he felt he could obtain maximum performance out of it that way. Gradually he acquired the knack of setting up the car almost as well as Jack, 'even if he never had a great deal of confidence in his own ability as test driver', according to Leo Mehl.

Jochen was second fastest during the first day of training at Zandvoort; the second day he was quickest but unable to equal Amon's pole position time of the previous day. For the race, he fitted dry-weather tyres, but it rained. On top of that the alternator broke, and although the battery was changed it was soon drained again, which robbed Jochen of any chance of finishing. Stewart scored Matra's first ever Grand Prix win.

Next came the Grand Prix of France at Rouen. Jackie Oliver's Lotus with its huge wing came to grief in practice, possibly as the result of turbulence during overtaking, and disintegrated when he lost control. Rouen is a real drivers' circuit, with fast, 130-mph corners which separate the men from the boys. After only seven practice laps, Jochen clocked fastest time of the day, 1.4 seconds quicker than Stewart. But he had little time to celebrate his first ever pole position. He had to dash back to his Paris flat to pick up mail and change his clothes. He had been so busy hurrying from place to place that he was still wearing his winter outfit.

'My practice time is almost too good to be true,' smirked Jochen. Unfortunately some vibrations developed in the untimed Sunday practice and they had to repair one of his fuel tanks. As usual I was sitting beside Jochen in the cab of the transporter while they tried to stop the leak. He had also lost a securing nut on his oil tank and the brakes were shot.

On race day the clouds were getting lower and darker and

Under Brabham's Wing

Jochen was faced with the agonising choice of which tyres to fit. Finally he decided to use the new all-weather tyres, but had to run these in during the opening laps of the race. Conditions were difficult, with a thin film of water covering the track. Later it was to pour down. After only 3 laps, Jo Schlesser left the track with the experimental new air-cooled Honda—Surtees had warned that he did not think this car was ready for racing. Schlesser's car hit the banking and burst into flames with over 50 gallons of high octane petrol on board. It was quite impossible to put out a fuel-fed fire. Charred or still burning debris littered the track; the other drivers were waved by the pillar of black smoke by officials. Sixteen drivers managed to squeeze through without trouble; Jochen was the one who didn't. His left rear tyre was punctured; after changing the wheel he fought his way back into sixth place, but a piece of metal from the wreck had punctured one of his fuel tanks.

'For ten long laps I sat soaked in petrol. I tried to hold on but it was impossible. It burned like hell.' In the 48th lap Jochen gave up and limped into the pits. His overalls were dyed red and streamed with moisture. Not knowing, he asked: 'Schlesser—is he dead?' The eyes of those around gave him the answer.

This was the fourth fatal accident to throw a shadow over the 1968 Grand Prix season. 'Schlesser's car was new and therefore probably not holding the road as well as it should, but Jo was an old hand, used to driving a wide variety of cars and after all, there isn't that much difference between Formula 1 and Formula 2,' was Jochen's opinion. 'In the case of Spence, Scarfiotti and Schlesser, I couldn't be absolutely sure whether it was a driving error or a mechanical fault.' Clark, Spence and Schlesser all crashed on the 7th of the month, and Scarfiotti on the 8th, while Lorenzo Bandini had died the previous year in Monaco, also on the 7th.

World War pilots used to claim they were only really sorry for those of their comrades killed in combat or in an accident;

Jochen Rindt

they showed contempt for those who were lost through over-confidence or thoughtlessness. Psychologists give us deep-rooted explanations as reasons why men drive and die in fast cars. They talk of heroic and suicidal attitudes, which they trace back to childhood and to exceptional mother-son relationships.

Jochen found it difficult to believe in heroic theories. 'People believe I must be as brave as a hero in a Western, but I get scared as easily as anyone else,' he used to say at that time.

Earlier, in 1965, he explained to me just what his attitude to moments of danger was: 'My philosophy is to think about it as little as possible.' A year later, after Peter Procter's blazing crash at Goodwood, he sat staring at the *Daily Mirror* with its sensational photos for minutes at a time. Bernie Ecclestone believes racing drivers don't think too much about their chances of fatal accidents, but the one thing they fear is fire and that, after all, is a very natural fear.

It was a good thing for Jochen that during this series of accidents he came under Brabham's wing; since Jimmy's death he could no longer simply forget about them.

To construct a car which allows for every possible mishap is impossible, but what can be done is to 'reduce the consequences of something happening and, even more basically, to try to prevent as far as possible that anything should happen in the first place. At Brabhams' I believe they succeed in doing this', Bernie summarised.

'A driver has neither the experience nor the opportunity of putting this into effect,' Jochen said. 'This means one has to rely on the team and this I can do. Of course, there is always the aim of making the car as light as possible. This is where I think some people, but not Brabham, go too far, as far as the strength of individual parts is concerned.'

Jochen reduced his racing programme drastically during 1968. No longer did he rush from a Saturday race in England to a Sunday event on the Continent, or enter in odd Por-

Under Brabham's Wing

sches or Alfa Romeos. He also lost interest in long-distance events, 'because they are boring and because the top drivers cannot really exert their full abilities. Nor do I consider it to be real racing if one has to obey team orders, like at Porsche'.

Rolf Stommelen was to come round to the same view later: 'At Porsche I was under military discipline, but with Brabham I had more freedom and could make my own decisions.' Brabham always had a soft spot for his 'lieutenants' and often gave them more than he took himself.

Although Jochen's year with Brabham was marred by unexpectedly bad luck, there was never any argument and not a harsh word was spoken. 'We never blamed one another, we just hoped from race to race and consoled ourselves that the next time everything would work, for sure.'

But it never did quite work out and, odd though it may sound, this had something to do with Brabham's splendid character.

CHAPTER TWELVE
Ford Intervenes

If you wanted to win Grand Prix races in 1968, you had to have a Ford V8 engine behind you, as was shown by the victories of Hill (Lotus), Stewart (Tyrrell-Matra) and Hulme (McLaren). There was Jacky Ickx's Ferrari win at Rouen, but that was the exception which proves the rule, due to a fantastic personal achievement in pouring rain, helped by his right choice of tyres. Brabham stuck to his Repco engine; these Australian power units had helped him to the world championship title in 1966 and did the same for his team mate, Hulme, in 1967. Brabham had been surprised they succeeded that year; while the engine was admittedly robust and reliable, it just didn't have enough horsepower. He had no illusions about his chances in 1968, especially in view of successful developments on the part of his rivals, and particularly Ford.

'So we carried on with our own development and tried to rush the four-camshaft engine through,' was the way Brabham described his predicament of 1968 to me. 'To be honest, the best solution would have been to have used Ford engines for that year and to have given Repco 12 months' grace, but after two successful years with them this would have been a very difficult decision. The car showed its true potential often enough, but the unreliability of the engines defeated us. Unfortunately the Repco works were 12,000 miles away, and things change too quickly in motor racing to cope with such a handicap.'

Ford Intervenes

During 1968 Brabham and Rindt between them used up five engines. 'None of them were completely destroyed; in fact they were all repaired, but the problems were serious enough to halt our cars.' The most frequent breakage occurred to the rocker arm between the camshaft and the valves; significantly this also happened to Jochen's Indianapolis engine.

Jochen knew his driving abilities qualified him for the world championship title. He knew he had the whole of the team behind him. He knew neither Brabham nor Tauranac nor the mechanics could be blamed that he had still not won a Grand Prix. He had largely overcome his starting nerves in spite of constantly unfavourable weather conditions; he had learned to judge the combination of weather, track, material and opponents. For him, there appeared only one solution: a Ford engine.

'We could have changed over to Ford engines halfway through 1968,' admitted Brabham. 'We considered and argued at length whether Jochen could gain enough world championship points at this late stage, but I finally decided against it because it wouldn't have been fair to Repco.' It was Jochen's misfortune that Brabham possessed this sense of loyalty. But Bernie told him: 'Without a sense of loyalty, it's not worth bothering about anything else. If you haven't got loyalty, there's not much left you can get.'

So the 1968 season drew to a close. The lack of success would have broken up any other team, especially one containing two such top-rank drivers, but it closed in friendship.

At Brands Hatch Jochen was the fastest in practice of all non-Firestone-shod cars. During the night before the race, part of the fuel injection system was changed for a new one which had been on the test bed. 'But during the warming-up lap the engine cut out completely between 7,500 and 8,500 revs and we could do nothing more before the start.'

Jochen struggled to retain eighth place, taking four seconds longer than during practice. 'The car ran dreadfully. Jack called me in and we worked on it. Although I stayed in eighth place the car was even slower, so the stop didn't help. Finally the fuel pump housing split and the car caught fire.'

The Grand Prix of Germany was run in dreary rain and fog. 'Today you're underpaid,' Tyrrell told Stewart before the start. Jochen was determined 'to drive to finish, taking it easy and safely . . . but as quickly as possible. Under conditions not entirely under my control I don't drive as fast as I can, but as fast as I consider sensible.' But because the performance of the cars is so similar, the competition is acute: 'If one is at the top one has to accept certain risks and I am prepared to do so.'

In this 'blind flying without radar' there was little opportunity for overtaking after the initial lap. Stewart—Hill—Amon—Rindt—Ickx read the order of the widely separated leading group, distinguished by Jackie's fantastic lonely drive in front. Jochen observed that the order corresponded with the quality of the rain tyres, i.e. Dunlop—Firestone—Goodyear.

Amon skidded off the track and so did Ickx, trying to pass Jochen, who summed up: 'I tried to follow the tyre tracks. If they had been largely washed away, I knew there was a gap ahead of me. If the tracks appeared still fresh I knew there was another car immediately ahead.' Hill's tyre tracks had almost disappeared, but not the ever-present danger, because 'Pokerface' had spun while Rindt approached at 150 mph. Luckily Graham had got the Lotus going by the time Rindt reached the spot. 'At that sort of speed you would need 300 or 400 yards to stop in the wet.' When Graham and Jochen passed the finish line for the last time but one, they were almost wheel to wheel, but Jochen didn't try to pass. 'It was impossible to overtake, at least not with any sense,' said Jochen when he finished; tired, exhausted, a little disappointed; 'so I only came in third.' Brabham incidentally was fifth—the only Grand Prix which he finished in 1968.

Water skiing

And just skiing

The wedding, Helsinki, 5th March, 1967

The Jochen Rindt Show, Vienna

Ford Intervenes

That evening, at the prize-giving in the Martini tent, Jochen appeared to be pleased when his prize money for third place was announced. But how important was money to him that year?

'I don't drive for money, but simply because I like driving. I don't drive better in a race where the financial rewards are higher, nor do I slacken off when the prize money is low. But racing without money, that would be like mountaineering without money; and I don't climb mountains for nothing. On the other hand I also try to save for the years when I shall not be driving any more.' In 1968 Jochen saw himself as a 'freelance artist'. He didn't count himself among the top earners but about halfway up the scale.

Graham Hill, racing in his 100th Grand Prix, lost a wheel at Monza. This incident, in the second part of the Lesmo curve, broke up the leading group. Twenty seconds behind the Ford-powered cars of Hulme, McLaren, Stewart and Siffert (of whom only Hulme was to finish) was a second bunch consisting of Rindt, Ickx and Servoz-Gavin. 'In the straights I had to take advantage of the slipstream; any passing I had to confine to the curves.' Jochen's race ended just before half-distance.

In Canada Rindt and Brabham decided to drive 'quite slowly in order to make absolutely sure of finishing', even though Jochen was fastest in practice. He was lying in second place, ahead of Hulme, the ultimate winner, and Brabham, who was fourth, when both Repco engines packed up once more. Watkins Glen brought merely a change of scenery; the result was the same. Then came Mexico.

I met Jochen, Nina, Bernie and his Chinese wife, Tuaina, for a few days of relaxation in that paradise on the Pacific, Acapulco. Surprisingly Jochen, a first-class sportsman on water, too, declined the chance of water-skiing: 'It costs a fortune here.' Instead he found a remote beach with huge breakers. The days passed in hammocks, and chewing coconuts; the evenings between Trans-Atlantic telephone calls

Jochen Rindt

and splashing in the hotel pool, the price of which was included in the $50-a-day tag of the bungalow hotel 'Las Brisas'.

Jochen wouldn't have been Jochen if he hadn't found some way of financing his holidays: he took his gin-rummy teacher Bernie for a cool $172. Bernie escaped to Mexico City, pleading that he found Acapulco much too hot; Jochen arrived a day later.

There are places along the Magdalena-Mixhuca course from which one can look over the wall into an Indian cemetery. The loudspeaker repeated the theme of *Vivre pour vivre*, and the first practice session coincided with All Souls' Day. It was truly a macabre ending to a season lined with crosses! Bernie thought Jack could qualify as a Mexican with his constant 'Manỹana, manỹana'. But although Brabham took the various delays and frustrations in his usual relaxed style, the determination for which 'Black Jack' is known showed through in practice, for he proved faster than Jochen for the first time in twelve Grands Prix.

Before the start Ron Tauranac taped ice cubes under Jochen's radiator: 'At least they'll last for the first few laps of the race.' On the 16th lap, Jochen failed to pass the pits and tension mounted. When Mexican driver Moises Solana drove by with his rear-wing in pieces, Nina started to cry, but Surtees calmed everybody down. Jochen had stopped on the track and was walking back. 'The ignition just packed up suddenly,' Jochen reported, and Nina, relieved, said: 'Give me a kiss.'

At least Jochen had a superb view of the duel between Hill and Stewart for the world championship; a duel which at times seemed to be in the hands of Walker-Lotus driver Siffert. 'I mustn't influence you, but it could depend on you whether Graham or Jackie becomes world champion . . .' is what Chapman whispered to Siffert before the start. But Seppi lost this opportunity by having to call at the pits. 'This is the right way to decide a world championship;

Ford Intervenes

Stewart and Hill were fighting it out,' Jochen said enthusiastically; he had reasons to wish both of them success. On the one hand Jackie was to open the Jochen Rindt Racing Car Show in Vienna; on the other Jochen would be joining Graham at Lotus for 1969. Stewart's fuel pump let him down and Hill became a convincing world champion. The mechanics said to him: 'You suddenly look twenty years younger, Graham; what happened?' Chapman was in tears as he embraced the mechanics.

As far as Jochen was concerned, his Mexican Grand Prix took place over the telephone. What he wanted was not a race, but a championship-winning car. 'Given the right car and a little bit of luck, I'd win the world championship hands down; even if this is no absolute criterion as to who is the best driver in the world.'

CHAPTER THIRTEEN

The Secret Grand Prix: Why Lotus?

However direct the initial confrontation between Aries Rindt (April 18th 1942) and Taurus Chapman (May 19th 1928), it was almost inevitable that they should come together. Several times during 1968 Chapman was heard to say that he could not imagine battling through 1969 with only Graham Hill at his disposal. He was looking for a new Jim Clark. 'Look over there and you'll see the most intelligent driver of today — and probably the best,' said journalist Elizabeth Hayward to Colin at Spa. Her finger pointed at Jochen. But Chapman had other ideas. 'For me, Mario Andretti is the driver of my dreams; he is probably one of the three best in the world. Later I asked him whether he would drive for me, were he to decide to spend a whole season in Europe.' Mario was doubtful in view of his USAC commitments; later he gave Chapman a definite 'no'. Thus Chapman approached Rindt at Brands Hatch in July. The discussions which followed didn't need a conference room; they took place amid petrol cans and oil drums or while catching a quick snack. 'Would you like to drive for me?' asked Chapman. It was not a question he put very often. There is no doubt that Chapman is the number one in the Grand Prix business. He's been around a long time, he can show the best balance sheet of success as well as a lot of glamour: he is 'Mr Motor Racing'. In the case of other teams the driver may knock at the door seeking a contract. With Chapman you don't approach him; he will talk to you, and this alone is quite

The Secret Grand Prix: Why Lotus?

an honour. Bernie considered Jochen had stuck out his neck long enough for relatively little reward; Jochen named his price and it was not a modest one.

'The driver tells me his conditions; I approach my sponsors, Gold Leaf, Firestone and Shell, and tell them: "We could get this man; he thinks he's worth that much." They say yes or no; in Jochen's case they all agreed in the affirmative and I went back to Jochen to tell him: "OK, we can go ahead."' That is how Chapman described the proceedings to me.

Then complete silence fell for a few weeks. Unexpectedly Andretti called again on Chapman. The situation had changed; 'I could drive eight or nine races for you after all.' Chapman decided he would be a fool to let Mario go to Ferrari; he also had the feeling Jochen wouldn't stay with Lotus for ever. Chapman therefore said 'yes' to Andretti as well: 'The last thing I wanted to do was to run a three-car team, but I was determined to have a place for Mario.' And if Chapman was playing a bit of a double game at this time, Jochen and Bernie were doing the same, for there were quite a number of alternatives open to Jochen.

There was, for example, the four-wheel drive car, still surrounded in secrecy, which Robin Herd had designed for Keith Duckworth. Preceded by paeans of praise, it was, according to rumour, destined for one of three teams: Tyrrell, for Stewart; Winkelmann, for Rindt; or, perhaps surprisingly, for John Surtees.

But this car never ran and very few ever saw it: 'When the wings arrived, Duckworth lost interest,' Robin Herd lamented later in explanation of the demise of his project.

More advanced was the Matra project. Jochen flew to Velizy to negotiate with Matra boss Lagadere, who suggested an arrangement similar to the one he had with Stewart; a Matra chassis free of charge, plus Ford engine and Dunlop tyres, with the driver's fee being looked after by the sponsor—in this case Winkelmann. As they had been a year earlier, the

Jochen Rindt

problems of running a private Formula 1 team were simply too great; above all there just wasn't enough money. Rindt estimated it cost £50,000 to set up a Formula 2 team. A Formula 1 team would be considerably more expensive; one Ford engine alone cost £7,500.

Alan Rees had great difficulty trying to find that sort of money. But Jochen kept the options open until the very last moment; the telephone wires from Acapulco to London became red hot. Jochen asked Bernie for advice, dangling his legs in the pool. 'If you leave things too long, the new season will start and you won't have a car at all,' Bernie said. 'Nor can you afford to devote another year to experiments. You must drive a car which can win races and which will give you the rewards you deserve. Lotus offers both.' In Mexico City, during practice, Jochen gave the Matra people his definite 'No'. This only left two alternatives: Lotus or Brabham.

'Jack, Ron and Leo Mehl really are the nicest trio in the whole business. If I do leave them, it will be with the greatest reluctance,' reflected Jochen. Jack tried everything to retain him; admittedly he still couldn't find the reason for the run of bad luck with the Repco engines, as the presumed cause of all the trouble with the camshafts still hadn't been established, but he was going to change over to Ford engines whatever happened.

Jochen told Brabham and Mehl quite frankly about the Lotus offer. 'We couldn't give him more than the equivalent of his earnings in Formula 2. And Chapman has considerable cash reserves including his own,' Leo calculated. Jack did his best to whip up some additional financial support and Jochen tried to find his own sponsors—but it still didn't amount to more than half of what Chapman was offering. And the Brabham and Goodyear people had the impression that, however much they offered, Chapman would outbid them. He was determined to buy the priceless gem which Rindt had now become to him and his offer was backed by substance.

The Secret Grand Prix: Why Lotus?

Up to the end of 1968, Lotus cars had won more Grand Prix races than any other make, except Ferrari in a much longer time—no less than 34, in fact. Lotus drivers gained three world titles (Clark in 1963 and 1965; Hill in 1968) while they lost two other championships by the narrowest of margins during the last races of the season (Clark in 1962 to Hill and in 1964 to Surtees). Morally Lotus could claim five world championships.

'If you look at it that way, you must concede that Chapman does always produce race-winning cars,' Bernie told Jochen. 'If you weigh it all up and if you take into account the money offered, it all seems to point to Lotus.' But Jochen continued to hesitate. If Brabham could only have reached 75% of the Lotus offer, Jochen would certainly have stayed with him. In any case Jack and Jochen agreed that they would drive together again one day. Said Jack: 'I like his style of living, his attitude to life: full of enthusiasm, keen, always ready to go, prepared to sally forth and do battle.'

'Considering I haven't won a single Grand Prix, I seem to play quite an important role,' Jochen noted with amusement in Mexico City. 'My parting from Brabham started a merry-go-round: if Surtees moves to Brabham, Ickx will stay at Ferrari; but if Surtees switches to BRM, Ickx will move to Brabham.' The second hypothesis came true: Ickx became Brabham's new lieutenant and Jack continued to drive himself. 'Had Jochen stayed with me, I would have given up,' he confided to me.

Over dinner in Mexico City's 'Richelieu', Nina told Jochen he was mad to drive for Lotus: 'You're much safer with Brabham.' Jochen agreed but felt he could not afford to forgo half his potential income. Slowly we walked up the Reforma to the 'Hilton'. 'Lotus will be my third team,' Jochen said to me thoughtfully. 'If I don't succeed there, I'll be finished. All teams are pretty much the same and one shouldn't change about too often. But at least I didn't lose anything by switching about.'

Jochen Rindt

Jochen was full of confidence: 'Lotus make the best cars, the most sensational ones and there isn't anything Chapman can't do, four-wheel drive, two-wheel drive—whatever I want. Technically speaking, I don't anticipate any difficulty.' But from a human point of view, I asked? 'Yes, this worries me. Chapman is a cool businessman. And Hill is World Champion. I realise Lotus never produce two equally good cars. On the other hand, I'm not their number two.'

A few days later, it was Chapman's turn to be upset. Jochen told him quite frankly that if he were to win the world championship, Colin could not expect big speeches from him. He would return to Geneva as quickly as possible. Colin shook his head: 'But Jochen, that's all part of being champion . . . but let's not worry about it now; we'll see what happens.'

CHAPTER FOURTEEN

Levin — An Upside Down Start

Jochen had to give up his habitual ski-ing holiday in Zürs during the winter of 1968-69. First he was entered for the Formula 2 Temporada, and then in the Tasman Series in New Zealand and Australia, his first races for Lotus. 'I always had absolute control over the Brabham, but in the Lotus it is impossible to make it do precisely what one wants; I feel like a passenger in it.'

Amon won the first Tasman round ahead of Jochen. At Levin there occurred the first sign of internal team rivalry when Jochen and Graham tangled their front spoilers during the preliminary heat. In the main race Jochen spun under braking, but in spite of proceeding cautiously he regained fourth place. Then there was more brake trouble, he spun again, hurtled backwards into an earth bank . . . and turned over.

'Don't worry, nothing happened and I'm fine,' Jochen told Nina over the telephone in order to forestall the newspapers. But Nina realised Jochen never talked about dangerous occurrences.

To use Chapman's words, the Levin incident was not due to 'ignorance' but to carelessness and human error: a mechanic had forgotten to replenish the brake fluid and the main reservoir was empty. 'The team was operating 10,000 miles from England,' Chapman explained. 'The boys go water ski-ing, lie on the beach and then rush back to the garage; this is bad, even diabolic, but what am I to do? First

Jochen Rindt

class mechanics are more difficult to get hold of than good drivers. Maybe I am too lenient but I try to be demanding and give them encouragement. Unfortunately they do forget something from time to time. Do you want me to get rid of this fellow here in Levin and ruin him completely? This would only make the others afraid to do anything at all.'

Chapman appreciated that these things could happen, but claimed he could always put them right. 'I hate the mechanics trying to hide something from me. This boy in Levin could have sworn on oath that he had filled the reservoir, that Jochen must have made a mistake and all that nonsense. But no: he came to me and admitted he forgot. I prefer that to a pack of lies.'

By now, Jochen felt pretty unhappy about the Lotus, and particularly about its reliability, for Graham was subjected to some defect in virtually every race. At Teretonga Nina arrived in time to see Jochen break a driveshaft on the start line. But Jochen still thought the Lotus to be a race-winning car: he won the Lady Wigram Trophy, won at Sandown Park and finished the series second only to Amon.

Together, Chapman and Rindt flew to their first Grand Prix, the South African, at Kyalami. The refuelling stop in Accra took place during a rainstorm. 'Colin and I ran across the tarmac to the first hut we could see. Inside we saw nothing but twenty white spots; they turned out to be ten Africans, staring at us,' remembered Jochen. When they arrived at Kyalami Jochen couldn't quite understand why Mario Andretti should be there, particularly as the team had no spare engine. 'Mine broke in practice and they gave me one of Alan Mann's, whipped out of a sports car,' Jochen complained. 'Why did Colin bring me down here when he already had two number one drivers, Andretti and Hill? He didn't need me at all, particularly as he had no engines.'

Chapman, too, was complaining: 'I have never had such a complicated driver. He is always demanding things!'

Levin—An Upside Down Start

That Jochen lapped quicker in practice than either Mario or Graham didn't seem to please him; nor that Brabham, now equipped with a Ford engine, obtained pole position. As expected, Jochen's engine let him down half-way through the race. Stewart won.

'At Brands Hatch Graham wouldn't let me pass. I complained to Colin and he stipulated that we must both permit the other to overtake. After that the relationship between Graham and me became more relaxed.' During the rainy International Trophy Race at Silverstone, Jochen's car dropped back for the first ten laps, due to a faulty electrical connection. Then he started to catch up and passed competitor after competitor, including Stewart; at the finish only one driver prevented him recording his first Formula 1 victory in a Lotus. Jack Brabham; it had to be him!

In the middle of March Jochen went to Barcelona on behalf of the Grand Prix Drivers' Association to check safety precautions, for the Montjuich Park was going to be the scene of the Spanish Grand Prix. Dated March 20th, Jochen submitted the following report to GPDA President Joakim Bonnier:

Begnins, 20 March 1969

Dear Joakim,

The organisers have shown me all they intend to carry out in the next five weeks, and I'm sure they are going to do everything humanly possible to make their circuit as safe as possible. The whole course will be enclosed by guard rails either side, except in the hairpin bends and those will have escape roads of satisfactory lengths (130 and 60 yards). In general, there are double guard rails on the outside of the track, single ones inside. However, I am not quite happy regarding the height of the single guard rails; their lower edge is only four inches above the ground, which seems too low; the entire rail is only hubcap high so that a car could easily tip over the top. I pointed all this out

Jochen Rindt

to the president, Mr Fabregas, who told me he had been given those measurements by the Monza director. But he is quite prepared to re-install the guard rails at any height we desire, as long as we can let him have the necessary dimensions within the next few days.

I didn't want to arrive at a decision on this point, as these dimensions are obviously laid down by the CSI. Would you therefore please phone him? The precise positions of the double guard rails are shown on the sketch of the track; in my view they have been placed correctly.

To complete it all, a nine foot high wire mesh fence has been erected by the Spaniards in all the more dangerous places, especially in front of the grandstands.

As you see, these people have accomplished a fantastic amount of work. A press conference was called after our discussions, and I gave due thanks and praise for everything they've done.

Please don't forget the matter of the guard rails.
With best wishes,
Jochen.

Jochen also corresponded with Lotus: about administrative matters (*I apologise for the Mr if you happen to be a girl,* reads the PS); about some additional insurance premium and about the new Formula 2 Lotus, the Mark 59. The outstanding quality of this car was its superb roadholding on fast circuits. Jochen took it to its first victory at Thruxton. Three days later Jochen sent Colin the following grateful 'fan' letter:

Begnins, 10 April 1969

Dear Colin,
Many thanks for urging your formula II department to get the car completed. It certainly helped; the car is first class and I would say it was pretty well the best handling car I've ever driven.

Should you require me for testing, I would like to do

this very much, especially the new formula I car. But do please give me a day's notice.

With best wishes,
Jochen.

Jochen also won at Pau, but in the third Formula 2 race of the season, for the Eifel Trophy on the Nürburgring, both his and Graham's car suffered steering arm failure at almost the same moment.

The Winkelmann team acted quickly: they reinforced the steering arms, and the rest of the front suspension, and thus avoided any further mechanical defect for the rest of the season. As some wheel nuts had worked loose early on, Pete Kerr secured them with a split pin: 'Perhaps not quite the thing to do but a useful safety measure; later other teams copied the idea.'

By early May, Jochen still hadn't signed his Lotus contract. 'He's still none too happy at Lotus, he basically doesn't want to drive for them,' recapitulated Bernie Ecclestone. 'Jochen waited till the last moment; had a deal with Brabham materialised after all, he would probably have signed with him.' Letters flew to and fro, but still no contract. Before he flew off to the Spanish Grand Prix, Jochen stuffed all the correspondence into his briefcase and passed it to Bernie: 'Here, you have the lot. Please deal with it and make sure the contract is perfect.'

Bernie got down to details with Colin in the latter's hotel room—Number 1201 in the 'Presidente'; Chapman telephoned briefly to his co-director, Mr Bushell, and then everything was in order. It should be added that Chapman always observed the terms of his agreement most punctiliously.

'If you had negotiated with Colin for another five minutes,' Jochen joked later, 'he would probably have sold you his factory as well.'

So in Barcelona Jochen finally appended his signature to his first Lotus contract, which, unless cancelled by either

Jochen Rindt

party before October 1st 1969, would continue automatically. In Paragraph 4 there was confirmation that Rindt was regarded as joint/equal Number One driver and that Lotus 'will do everything to produce for him suitable and appropriate cars'.

Under Paragraph 11, Section 2, Rindt agreed that if he suffered injuries of whatever nature, whether fatal or not, in a vehicle manufactured, owned or controlled by Lotus, then he absolved the company, its employees, associates and agents, from any blame whatever. This is the usual renunciation which is insisted upon in more or less similar terms in all Formula 1 works contracts. In the same paragraph, Section 3, Rindt agreed to accept all race instructions given to him by the team manager 'in the interests of the team and its drivers'.

In the next paragraph Jochen agreed to share all trophies and prizes on an equal 50-50 basis. Any prize money was to be shared in the normal fashion, that is 45 per cent for the team, 45 per cent for the driver and 10 per cent for the mechanics. The bonuses paid by the accessory firms were split equally between team and driver; the mechanics do not benefit in this respect in any Formula 1 team except McLaren. Bruce had rather unusual and generous views regarding the morale of his staff.

CHAPTER FIFTEEN

Barcelona

'For me, every day I drove for Brabham felt like Christmas.' Jochen was unable to feel the same a year later with Lotus. During the first day of practice at Barcelona he was unable to avoid a dog; on the second a shock absorber broke and on the third he was delayed by a cracked brake disc.

Daily, it seemed, the rear wing of the Lotus 49 continued to grow. 'Now it's as wide as the car, right to the outside edge of the tyres,' Jochen noted with concern, 'and they had to cut the corners off the front spoilers because they fouled the wheels.' Team Lotus participated in the aerofoil epidemic to the full; Chapman even loaned aluminium parts to McLaren. How much the wings grew seemed to depend on how much material each team could find for the purpose!

'I'm determined to see complete success for Jochen and Graham. Our cars are relatively old, two years, and I'm convinced we can obtain better performance by using larger wings,' said Chapman. Promptly Jochen accomplished by far the fastest practice lap. 'When Jack was told, he gasped,' reported a cheerful Bernie Ecclestone, helping out in the Brabham pit. 'I am satisfied,' Jochen said, 'but I also know who is going to provide my principal headache tomorrow: Stewart!'

May 4th started cloudy and rainy, but the sun came out just before the start. While London fashion photographer Clive Arrowsmith was busy shooting the photos still to be seen today on Rindt posters, Jochen squatted on the crash

Jochen Rindt

barrier. 'Clive asked me to tell Chapman the door of his Lotus Elan rattles. . . . But Chapman doesn't seem to listen when I tell him things aren't right on the Lotus 49!' Jochen appeared relaxed, remote from problems; Stewart likened it to the effect of a deflating balloon. 'We let ourselves be drained of all emotions before the start, like all the air escapes from a balloon if you prick it with a pin.'

Jochen shot away to a picture start. He drew away from Chris Amon's Ferrari by about a second a lap. For the first time since the watersplash at Spa in 1966, Jochen was actually leading a Grand Prix. On the ninth lap he automatically registered the waving yellow flags in the left-hander past the pits, and immediately afterwards he recognised the shunted remains at the side of the track with only one wheel left in place; left rear.

Jochen knew it was Graham Hill's Lotus. What he couldn't know was that Graham's rear wing support had broken immediately after the hump-back. Even Graham didn't realise it as yet; all sorts of things could have broken. He had just survived an agonising crash and was busy pushing the debris as close to the guard rail as possible; he had no time to analyse the cause of the accident.

'I tried for several laps to communicate with Graham by means of hand signals, but as I didn't get any response, I assumed that I was in no danger. Nor did the pits give me any signals.' Then Dave, Hill's mechanic, ran across, on Chapman's instructions, to find out what had happened. When he got to Hill's car, Dave thought he could see the beginnings of a fracture in Rindt's wing but he wasn't sure: it could have been an illusion. Hill had the same suspicion. He sent Dave back to the pits to warn Chapman; he should order Jochen in.

But it was too late. On the 20th lap, also after the hump-back and at a speed of about 140 mph. Jochen's right-hand wing gave way. The aerofoil bent back, and this resulted in the lifting effect which Jochen had always feared:

Jochen's Lotus takes off during the Spanish Grand Prix at Barcelona, 4th May, 1969

Barcelona, 1969: Jochen car hurtles towards the remains of Graham Hill's car

Graham Hill trying to extricate Rindt

Spanish police by the wreckage of the two cars

Barcelona

the rear of the car rose up and appeared to climb the guard rails, which had fortunately been raised on Jochen's insistence a few weeks earlier; the car was thrown to the right, collided with the remains of Hill's Lotus, turned over and slid along the track upside down.

Graham's 'golden hands', which had rescued the trapped Stewart at Spa in 1966, now came to Jochen's immediate assistance. Petrol was running everywhere in enormous quantities; the smallest spark could have started an inferno. Jochen's face was bleeding badly, but he was conscious and muttered: 'Shit.'

When Stewart passed the next time he saw Jochen moving on the stretcher. 'For me that was good enough, but suddenly I couldn't see Graham any more; instead I saw a marshal place a finger on his throat—which presumably meant someone had been killed; I was afraid it might be Graham, for I had seen Graham kneeling by his car before Jochen crashed.'

Stewart only learned the welcome truth after he finished first, thanks largely to the retirement of Amon and Siffert; a win 'in the worst race I ever drove in; I felt as if I had stolen both the race and the victory.'

They took Jochen, suffering from concussion, a broken nose and a broken jaw, to the private clinic run by Professor Soler-Roig. Nina was allowed in first, then Bernie, then me. 'I'm through with racing, I'll retire,' Jochen told Nina; then he asked Bernie, 'Did you get hold of my starting money?'—a question which made Jackie Stewart, waiting in the lobby, laugh for the first time that day: 'Bloody Jochen doesn't change.' As Chapman and Hill had returned to England, Stewart undertook to charter an executive jet to fly Jochen back to Geneva. They informed Jochen accordingly, but when he found out the cost—£500—he decided: 'Much too expensive, I'll take the ordinary tourist flight.' Having noted the time, he realised he had missed the flight anyway and dropped off to sleep. Next to her roses Nina placed the trophy Jochen had won for fastest lap. Jochen rejected congratulations, pointing out that Stewart was over 18 points ahead in the world championship. During his five days in the clinic he did a lot of thinking, but any thoughts about retirement soon receded and Nina told me privately: 'I can't beg Jochen to stop racing. He would hate me for the rest of his life.'

Accident photos in the Spanish press quite upset Jochen. He felt Graham should have stopped him; that he had failed to do so was to rankle for a long time. Bernie pointed out that Graham couldn't have known. 'What would you have thought if he had tried to stop you when you were leading a Grand Prix for the first time in three years?' 'Well, Colin should have stopped me,' countered Jochen, but Bernie argued: 'How would you have reacted if there had been no sign of any defect in your wing? I certainly wouldn't have brought you in.'

When I did a radio interview on Monday Jochen was able to remember the crash in every detail: 'But at the very moment of impact one doesn't do anything. One observes what is going on, rather like a third party. A broken off wheel, or even a collapsed suspension, would have given me more of a chance. And if they hadn't doubled the height of the guard rails, I wouldn't be alive now. I owe President Fabregas a debt of gratitude. I know they cost a fortune, but surely everyone will now realise that at certain places around any track there must be these barriers. Without them I feel certain . . . it's highly probable . . . there would be two fewer Grand Prix drivers.' Jochen talked fluently but his voice had an apathetic sound; stubborn and full of helpless anger.

On Monday evening Jochen was dozing off when he mumbled to Nina: 'I always wondered what Jimmy felt at Hockenheim. Now I think I know: nothing.'

Stewart confirmed from his own experience that there is no fear, no feeling, nothing at the time of the accident; the pain, often severe pain, comes later. 'I think that is

Barcelona

the reason why none of us seriously consider chucking it in after an accident. A certain shock remains. I know of virtually no top driver who hasn't been involved in an accident; in fact I consider it a necessary part of climbing the ladder of experience—not that an accident is desirable in itself, but it serves to emphasise you are not indestructible. You appreciate there may be other accidents unless you think ahead. As a result you don't drive any slower but you become aware of certain conditions which should be avoided, which may result in an accident.'

The Friday after Barcelona, Jochen returned to Lake Geneva. He asked his friend, Viennese jeweller and former sports car driver Gotfrid Kochert, to design a special present for the Automobile Club of Catalonia: it was to be a gold plated, double height guard rail with the inscription: *With sincere thanks, Jochen Rindt,* all mounted on a stone base.

Chapman's initial thoughts on his way home from Spain were to withdraw from Monaco, but he soon changed his mind. Hectic activity at his Hethel factory rebuilt two older cars and these were speedily prepared for Monaco, to be driven by Hill and Attwood.

Jochen now wrote to all the principal British motoring magazines with a view to getting the 'death wings' banned; the only one which didn't print it was *Motor Sport*. Denis Jenkinson considers today's drivers are reared on milk and water and are too concerned with their own safety. He is quoted as saying at the time: 'I would have accepted the opinion of Hill or of Brabham, but Rindt hasn't even won a Grand Prix, and I'll bet my beard he never will.' The CSI announced the ban on wings during the first practice session at Monaco. Jochen saw Hill win, followed by Courage, Siffert and Attwood—three Lotus-Fords in the first four —on the TV screen in Bonnier's house. 'He sat there with all his former enthusiasm, shouting encouragement for Piers Courage in second place,' Nina said. When I rang him from Monte Carlo Jochen mused as if to himself: 'I seem to be

Jochen Rindt

Catastrophe Charlie of every team. I always drive at the wrong time, in the wrong car and in the wrong race.' During practice at Indianapolis Andretti's Lotus lost a wheel; Mario escaped with a graze on his face. 'The heat treatment of the wheel nuts had not been carried out correctly,' Chapman told me. 'Although new parts arrived in time to qualify, there was no time for Jochen and Graham to do any testing.' Chapman's subsequent decision to withdraw the cars was warmly welcomed by Jochen as he didn't want to drive an untried car. It was a decision which cost Colin Chapman £70,000 to £80,000, as well as creating a host of problems with Firestone.

CHAPTER SIXTEEN

Mr Motor Racing
— Colin Chapman

To many, Anthony Colin Bruce Chapman looks like David Niven's double: the same sort of moustache, the same casual elegance. 'He's smaller than the film star but nevertheless of very elegant appearance' was Jochen's early impression of him. Chapman habitually wears peaked caps; when he takes them off a wreath-like impression remains in his hair.

After retiring from the RAF as a pilot in 1948 he used his savings from his work days with the British Aluminium Company to start work on his own in a converted stable in Alexandra Park Road, North London. Twenty-five pounds he borrowed from Hazel, later to be his wife and partner. He commenced by converting old Austin Sevens, and shortly afterwards he gave the firm the name Lotus. He has certainly come a long way since then. In 1959 the works moved to Cheshunt, and in 1966 to a new £350,000 factory at Hethel in Norfolk. It's three hours by car from London Airport to Hethel but only 25 minutes by air in Colin's 'Navajo', at the controls of which he spends over 350 hours each year.

The home of the Lotus blossom is a light-brown brick building. Everywhere there are glass-fibre bodies and backbone chassis. Production engines are run for 30 minutes on a bank of test beds; subsequently each car undergoes a test run on Lotus' own proving track before leaving the factory. They can produce 100 cars a week. Yearly production quadrupled between 1964 and 1969, and reached 4,506 cars, with a turnover of £5,290,000, in the latter year; this was all built on racing successes. Today, Group Lotus is worth over £5,000,000.

'During the last ten years I have received take-over offers at regular intervals,' Chapman confided to me, 'but I prefer to run Lotus myself.' He is of course a millionaire, 'but my so-called wealth exists only on paper, not in cash. If Lotus ever ran into difficulties, I would be the main sufferer. People believe that because I'm successful in business and in motor racing, I must spend all my time chasing after money. This is not the case: I enjoy adventure and success; I was always a gambler. Success in business is measured financially; success in motor racing by victories.' Faced with a choice between business or racing, Chapman 'would always go for the sport'.

And he takes part in motor racing in order to win; he is not interested in just finishing. 'Only when we have won do I look up to see just how much money this has earned us or how many world championship points we have gained. All that comes afterwards. First I want to win.' For the same reason, Chapman considers the championship points system unrealistic: 'The championship should go to the driver with the largest number of victories and not the one with the most points.'

Chapman and his mechanics get really annoyed when rivals start snooping around their cars and knowingly pointing out parts which, in their opinion, are too weak. 'We don't go round criticising others.' It has always been Chapman's burning ambition to be ahead in design, to be the leading constructor. 'We constantly try to introduce new ideas but unfortunately they don't always work out.' As far as Ford of Europe Vice-President Walter Hayes is concerned — and he pulls most of the strings in Formula 1 — 'There is little doubt that Colin is one of the few true geniuses in the world of motor racing.'

Mr Motor Racing — Colin Chapman

Jochen felt most unhappy after the Barcelona accident. Subconsciously he tended to reject Chapman's money. Basically his requirements were quite modest; naturally he wanted to earn as much as anyone, but he had little personal use for money. He rarely bought anything for himself. He had two jersey shirts, a green one and a blue one, and he wore them alternatively for just about every occasion. Nina had quite a job to convince him that the expensively and colourfully dressed Stewart didn't look like a Court Jester, as Jochen imagined. Piers Courage, too, who favoured wide Carnaby Street ties, began to have some influence on Jochen's attitude to fashion.

Of course, Jochen was building a house for himself, but he would never have tried to make money just in order to build a big house with five bedrooms and three bathrooms. He happened to have the money and he needed a house; that was his order of priority in such matters.

One thing was certain. Jochen knew he hadn't slowed down as a result of the accident. He made his come-back in the Formula 2 race at Zolder and won it convincingly. 'Colin needs me more than I need him,' Jochen considered, as he could have swapped horses at any time. He often talked to Jack Brabham, and Nina believes they discussed the possibility of Jochen returning to the Brabham team. But Jochen opposed any breach of contract, which would, incidentally, have been far more serious a matter than in earlier years: 'I must finish what I've started.' Jochen saw it all in black and white; full involvement or none at all; there was no halfway solution. Similarly, if Jochen wanted to let someone know he didn't like him, he had little difficulty in doing so. (From Zandvoort onwards, the 'endearments' flew both ways.)

Rindt was the first-ever non-British Team Lotus driver; as far as Chapman was concerned he was 'the first foreigner and, as such, very different from the British character.' But that wasn't really the point. Jacky Ickx had this to say about Jochen: 'Obviously he's not looking for sympathy from anyone, but he reveals himself as an extremely likeable personality if you are prepared to take the trouble to get to know him.' And Chapman made the comparison: 'Jim Clark was calm and an introvert, while Jochen was outspoken and terribly, terribly blunt.'

Only after mid-season did I see Colin and Jochen sit down together for a meal. Chapman's initial impression was of 'a whole entourage around Jochen; Richard Burton, seeking to be appointed his manager; that fashion photographer; and all sorts of longhaired friends. For reasons best known to him, he just doesn't want to become a member of the team. I had quite a different relationship with my other drivers; Jimmy and I spent much of our time together even away from the racetrack—but OK, if this is what Jochen wants, it's all right with me. I notice in other teams, too, the drivers don't always want to eat with their team bosses.'

Like a soldier, Graham Hill obeyed orders and was prepared to drive any car Chapman allocated to him. Jochen tried to adopt a more cautious attitude, especially in the case of the wedge-shaped, four-wheel drive Lotus 63, which Chapman revealed for the first time at the Dutch Grand Prix: 'I was none too keen on this car because I was of the opinion that a brand new model shouldn't be tested during official practice. McLaren, Stewart and Courage had already spent three days here, but not us. In Barcelona the Lotus 49 showed it was still capable of winning; why do we have to risk experimenting?'

Jochen declined to drive the Lotus 63. For Chapman it was a new experience to have somebody standing up to him. Stewart thought only Rindt could do this.

Jochen had found a newspaper with a photo of Graham's Barcelona crash and held it up, saying: 'This was my car' —which basically it was, although with some small differences. Passing the Volkswagen garage near the beach later on, he came across a sign *Bargain, for sale* which he removed from a Volkswagen and placed on the nose of the Lotus 63.

Jochen accomplished fastest practice time with the 49. Just five minutes before the start of the race itself his battery was found to be flat and was replaced; he took the lead from Stewart and gained a second a lap on him: the same Rindt-Lotus show as in Barcelona! But this time it lasted for only 16 laps or 22 minutes, six less than in Spain. Without being stressed, and not under the strain of acceleration, the right rear knuckle joint gave up just in front of the pits.

'I am sorry,' Chapman commented and crossed out entry number two. 'Thus was set the pattern for my Grand Prix season,' Rindt complained. 'Stewart will win again with a total of 27 points to his credit. We've lost two dead cert wins, and things won't always go as smoothly in practice as they have done so far.'

A few days later, while engaged in tyre testing at Silverstone, Jack Brabham had the misfortune to break his left ankle, and this put him out of action until Monza. Jochen and Nina sent him a get-better-quickly letter.

Clermont-Ferrand was to be the first race for the Lotus team in which Jochen's failure to win could definitely be blamed on personal rather than technical reasons: 'If anyone ever suffered from car sickness it would be here,' Stewart commented about this race track in the Auvergne mountains. The intense heat, the stifling cockpit and the 51 corners per lap, with an altitude difference of over 500 feet, combined to knock out Jochen, who hated racing in hot weather anyway and was still suffering from the consequences of his accident at Barcelona. During practice he had to stop every two laps to be sick. Piers Courage was concerned – 'Is he ill?' – and lent him his open-type helmet; the light blue one with the Eton emblem. Later, in the cool of the evening, Jochen was able to go four seconds faster.

Two cracks developed in Hill's steering column during final training; not until the following morning did they

Jochen Rindt

discover the same defect in Jochen's car. Chief mechanic Dick Scammell arranged to weld in a new section. Jochen learned of this only by accident when Piers Courage chanced to mention it. Jochen had a look and commented calmly: 'If that doesn't last, I shan't be coming back.' Then he smiled, 'Not to worry.'

Stewart told me he intended to return to Geneva immediately after the race and wanted to know when Jochen would be leaving. He'll decide at five, I told him. 'Or perhaps as early as a quarter past three,' Stewart quipped. Jochen sauntered to the start, deep in thought. 'Try to stay in the race,' Chapman pleaded. During the drivers' briefing, Jochen and the others were asked to keep to the right in case of any accident, as ambulances and service vehicles would drive on the left.

'It only took five laps before I started to feel sick again,' Jochen explained later. 'For as long as I felt reasonably fit I battled with Ickx, but then I had to let him past—and Beltoise too. For some time I managed to stay in fourth place. But from lap 12 onwards I wanted to give up.' Five laps later Jochen had slowed to 3 minutes 10 seconds, and continued losing another second each lap.

'Increasingly I lost all feeling of balance, and I couldn't even go flat out on the straights. I reacted too late for the corners, I drove like a drunk, and I began to feel weaker and weaker . . . suddenly I had a mental picture of Bandini. He started to feel unwell during the race at Monaco; I felt unwell before I even started.'

Jochen suffered for 69 minutes 31.4 seconds; then he coasted into the pits and dragged himself to the wall. 'I could kill myself . . . Sorry,' he said to Chapman, who replied with a friendly: 'That's all right.'

Stewart won his best race of the season but the chequered flag gave him little joy, only relief: 'Jesus Christ, what a way to earn a living!' That night thunderstorms raged in the area between Clermont-Ferrand and Lake Geneva, and Jochen was sick again during the trip home.

Mr Motor Racing — Colin Chapman

Team Lotus finally divided into two camps during the British Grand Prix at Silverstone: on the one side Chapman; on the other Rindt and Hill.

Team Lotus would field no less than four cars for the race. 'Lotus is like the biggest circus in the world. We work in troupes like at Barnum and Bailey,' Jochen joked grimly. He rolled tyres along and helped where he could in order to reduce the chaos caused by the four-car team. Miles and Bonnier would drive Lotus 63s; Rindt and Hill Lotus 49s, Bonnier having lent Hill the car he had just purchased.

'We always try to run too many cars and overwork the mechanics,' Jochen warned. He achieved pole position after Stewart had slit one of his tyres on a strip of concrete and crashed at Woodcote; number one Matra looked sadly bent.

Jochen had trouble with the starter just before the five minute signal: 'Good luck, Jochen,' Chapman gave him a little tap on the crash helmet. 'I hope the engine will fire.' With that Colin disappeared in the direction of the other drivers. 'He has a long way to go,' muttered Jochen. Hill had only managed the sixth row, and Miles the seventh.

Rindt and Stewart left the line as if obsessed; for the first time they were able to compare their performance directly. 'My Lotus seemed a shade faster, but the Matra held the road better and gained about ten yards braking for most of the corners.' Jochen broke the lap record for the Silverstone circuit three times; Stewart, beginning to realise that this looked like being Jochen's first Grand Prix win, shattered it six times.

'Most people believe Jochen is on the ragged edge while Jackie drives coolly and calmly,' Bruce McLaren observed. 'Yet when they both lapped me, the reverse applied.' In this Silverstone duel Rindt led the first six laps, Stewart took over from lap 7 to 15, and then Rindt was out in front until lap 61.

But suddenly his mirror confirmed the worst: by this time the rear wing was low down and was firmly anchored

Jochen Rindt

to the chassis, but the left-hand end-plate had broken and was chafing the tyre. Rindt rushed into the pits; the mechanics couldn't find any tin shears and pulled the thing off with their bare hands.

Although now 35 seconds down on Stewart, Rindt still lay second in the race that should have been his. In fact Ickx, McLaren and Courage hadn't even come into sight, but 6 laps before the end Jochen arrived in the pits once more with a set face and a stuttering engine: he was out of fuel. Hill and Siffert, the other two Lotus 49 drivers, were to encounter the same misfortune in the 80th and 81st laps.

The refuelling took ages, almost two eternal minutes. Millions of TV viewers saw the agonies of the exhausted, overworked Lotus mechanics, and fumed in sympathy with Rindt. 'There's only one thing; if one is lucky enough to have one's bad luck seen by so many, one can't really be that unlucky.'

Rindt now battled with his friend Piers Courage for fourth place, but then the latter's engine began to cut out. Williams gave him a sign 'LL SLOW' – 'Last Lap, drive slowly to save fuel' – and thus Jochen came in fourth. Two pit stops destroyed all real hope of finally overcoming the jinx from which he had suffered so long. Rindt had become a tragic, Hemingway-like character of Grand Prix racing.

Courage was hardly out of the cockpit before he started yelling at Williams: 'What sort of team manager do you think you are? You've cost me a place!' Frank, whose caution was no doubt justified, shouted back that he could find a new driver any time. It was an embarrassing scene. But it was nothing compared with the scene in the Lotus pit. 'I'm so sorry,' Chapman said to Nina; she just turned on her heels and marched off.

Lotus didn't fill up with enough petrol either because the hectic practice period didn't allow them time for calculations or because someone simply poured in one drum too few. Chapman came up with a precise explanation: 'Jochen had quite enough fuel in his tank but the petrol pump couldn't cope. The fuel system in the Lotus 49 is terribly complicated. It can happen that there are five gallons in the tank but the pump doesn't pick it up. Jimmy lost first place at Monza in 1967, and with it his world championship title, for exactly the same reason.'

Jochen left Silverstone by helicopter; he missed Graham Hill's traditional British Grand Prix party at 32 Parkside, Mill Hill.

CHAPTER SEVENTEEN

Decision for Lotus

'I feel my bad luck is destroying me,' Jochen told me that summer. His bad luck affected him as much as the atmosphere in the team. 'Chapman and I only seem to argue with one another now.' The moment Jochen started to talk to Chapman, the conversation disintegrated into nothing. He therefore took to phoning Bernie Ecclestone whenever he had to say anything to Chapman, and Bernie thereupon telephoned Wymondham 3411. When they arrived at the Nürburgring, both Rindt and Chapman realised that things just couldn't go on. For three hours they squatted in the transporter; they even missed half the Friday morning practice. Chapman showed Jochen a huge photo of him in an English newspaper, caption *Is this man the perfect race driver?* 'Don't you believe it, Jochen, you're far from it. You're fine in the car, but you're a bastard outside.'

Jochen would be the last to expect hymns of praise. 'Perhaps I shouldn't talk so much. Certain matters should be confined to the team. But when one suffers so much misfortune, hard words come easily.'

Chapman was also prepared to concede some points that day in the transporter: 'I admit I sold those 49s rashly and that we overworked the mechanics.' But Chapman would not admit that it was 'a hell of a business', as Jochen put it, to share being number one at Lotus. 'My former number two always had the same car as Clark,' he insisted.

Nevertheless he offered Jochen a privileged position for

Decision for Lotus

1970; the full Clark 'service'. 'If you stay with me, you alone will be my number one next year. Graham will have his own car, because I can't just kick him out after twelve years, and I'll find you a number two. But all our efforts will be concentrated on you.' Jochen promised to think it over. 'All right; I'll go ahead and organise a Rob Walker contract for Hill,' Colin said.

When Jochen finally commenced his much-delayed practice runs he soon broke the 8-minute barrier. 'Anyone faster?' he asked Chapman. 'Of course,' the boss replied, 'Stewart!' — but the 'of course' referred to Jackie's Dunlop tyres, not to any indication of driver quality.

For Jochen the day was completely overshadowed by Gerhard Mitter's fatal accident. To Jochen, pondering deeply, it was a crash he should have survived, one which was difficult to explain. That evening I attended the Lotus party held at Bernkastel on the Moselle with Jochen, Chapman, Hill and Andretti. Chapman was at his charming best, chatting and serving food. I turned to Jochen: 'In a year or two you'll both be saying "We used to hate each other but now we're the best of friends."' Jochen almost shouted his reply: 'Me stay at Lotus? I couldn't imagine it.' Jochen dropped out with engine trouble during the race. When Chapman turned to Nina and told her he had disappeared from the leader board, Nina complained: 'He'll never make it.'

'It takes luck to drive for the right team in the right year,' Jochen concluded matter-of-factly; one reason why he thought he would be parting with Lotus was the trump card he had up his sleeve for 1970. The trail led to Robin Herd, as it had three times before; the initial discussions had begun early in 1969.

The basic idea was this: Robin was to leave Cosworth and design two cars with the sole objective of gaining the world championship for Rindt in 1970. One car was to be four-wheel drive and the other two-wheel drive, to be used according to the nature of the track and the weather. Jochen

Jochen Rindt

and Bernie proposed to finance this gigantic operation themselves and to reward Robin generously into the bargain. 'As for the sponsors, we won't look for any until we start winning,' Bernie said.

Jochen, Bernie and Robin were to share all profits equally. Bernie turned this down: 'You take 45 per cent each, I'm happy with 10 per cent.' On top of that Rindt was to have a salary of £35,000 a year and Herd £10,000. Robin considered this most generous and gave his word on the deal.

At the Nürburgring Jochen showed me the publicity brochures which had already been designed and which were to bring in the supporting finance. Under an enormous photo of Jochen there was the caption *The fastest man in the world*, which Jochen amended to *The fastest man in Grand Prix racing*; there was also a fascinating biography of Robin Herd, headed *The man who had to succeed*.

From the Ring Jochen flew to Spain to see Alex Soler-Roig, who wanted to share in the project. In the meantime the situation in England became increasingly confused for Jochen. One of the conditions laid down was that Herd, subject to Rindt's agreement, should appoint the team manager. Alan Rees was chosen, but he involved two friends in the project: Max Mosley—son of the politician Sir Oswald Mosley—and businessman Graham Coaker.

It began to dawn on Jochen that too many cooks were spoiling the broth. Mosley, Rees and Coaker wanted to build Formula 1, Formula 2 and Formula 3 cars in quantity. Herd also entered into commitment with them—perhaps with his family responsibilities he preferred the long-term prospects of a manufacturing concern. Using the initial letters of the names Mosley—Alan—Rees—Coaker—Herd, MARCH was born!

Quite put out, Jochen flew to Finland to join Nina's parents. He also had a meeting with Teddy Mayer, McLaren's business manager, and Leo Mehl, Goodyear's racing chief. They wanted him to join the McLaren team because Bruce wanted

Jochen and Nina in Switzerland

Flying Lotus 49: Nürburgring, 1969

Rindt in the cockpit: Clermont Ferrand, 1969

Decision for Lotus

to retire from Formula 1. However, Jochen wouldn't sign without participating in the dollar-rich Can-Am series and the talks broke down.

Next Matra talked to Jochen, and then Ferrari's racing chief Mauro Forghieri approached him. But most important of all, Jack Brabham made another offer for Rindt to return to his team, as he felt his cars were back on form and it might be worthwhile for Jochen to think in those terms.

But in the meantime Rindt and Chapman had got to know and understand each other a lot better. 'Jochen made it very difficult for me to get to know him, but when one does finally get under his skin one discovers a heart of gold,' Chapman told me in the 'Hotel de la Ville' at Monza, while eating his way through their entire inventory of patisseries. 'It has taken me a year. Jochen's outstanding characteristic is his complete honesty in everything he thinks and says, and I have learned to respect this.'

In particular Chapman was 'pleased and grateful' that Jochen had tried the four-wheel drive Lotus after all: he had driven it in the Gold Cup race at Oulton Park, and had finished second to Ickx. To study its behaviour in the corners Chapman had lain spreadeagled on the ground. 'In this one hour I learnt more about four-wheel drive than during thousands of miles of testing. One point which Jochen couldn't understand was this: new cars have to be tested under actual racing conditions, not just in tests.'

Jochen was now reconsidering his position with Lotus, 'because the car is first-class, because there are many advantages to being with Lotus'. During practice at Monza he discovered that he could get an extra 300 revs down the straight without his rear wing, but he decided to put it on again quickly so that the others would not realize what he was up to.

During the final practice session silence descended on the autodrome. The public address system had no more times to announce, and all the drivers hung around, yawning, in

Jochen Rindt

their pits; they had postponed their chase after fractions of seconds to the last half hour, to take advantage of the cooler weather. They were like front-line soldiers waiting for the dawn attack, not knowing from which direction it would come. 'The hour of the slipstream battle is approaching,' Jochen told Bette Hill with a big grin.

Stewart waltzed over: 'I see you're using the wing again — but yesterday without?' Jochen feigned surprise. Jackie waggled his finger: 'I saw you, Rindt; I saw it all.' Stewart explained to me that there came a point when the drivers no longer talked about their cars; you rarely found Jackie and Jochen discussing mechanical problems. 'You had to tell little lies — and why should one lie?' Stewart asked.

Quite a few drivers believe that you need two slipstream tows at Monza, one past the pits and another at the far side of the track, between the second part of Lesmo and the Parabolica. 'Two really experienced drivers can pull one another along as if linked with a rubber band, as long as they don't hold each other up in the corners,' Jochen thought. He made a slipstreaming assistance pact with Piers Courage: 'You go out first, Piers. I'll try to catch you up and then pass you; if you can't hang on, I'll slow down for you.' The 'rubber band' is effective up to 250 yards.

But Hulme and McLaren latched on to Courage and Rindt and this altered the grid positions: first row, Rindt and Hulme; second row, Stewart and Courage; third row, McLaren and Beltoise. A speck of dust got into Jochen's eye; Chapman fished it out.

It had taken Stewart two days to find the right gear ratios for the sprint from the Parabolica to the start/finish line — but Jochen was quite unhappy after five laps: 'At first, fifth gear was much too low; I was on the rev limiter before I reached the finish line.' With inches between them the leading pack tore round the track. 'Most motorway dicers would be amazed how fairly and correctly we drive in Formula 1,' Jochen often used to say. 'With possibly two or three ex-

Decision for Lotus

ceptions.' These exceptions soon retired or found themselves right at the back. Courage led the race on several occasions, the first and only time he was ever to do so, but then he dropped back. The final battle was fought out by Stewart, Rindt, Beltoise and McLaren. On the last lap Rindt led at Lesmo, though he didn't realise it was the last lap because he didn't see either the official leader board or the Lotus pit signal. At the Parabolica Beltoise forced his way through and Stewart moved alongside him—'Which meant that Jochen could not come in,' was how Jackie put it. Jochen slipped past Beltoise on the finishing straight and was catching Stewart inch by inch, passing him only 25 yards after they had crossed the line. Winning by 8/100ths of a second, Stewart was now finally and irreversibly confirmed as world champion. The Dunlop transporter was almost swept away by thousands of wild fans; some distance away Jochen, drained of emotion and dirt-encrusted, signed autographs.

'Jackie is 6:0 ahead of me in the matter of wins, but it could just as well have been 3:3 or 4:2,' Jochen pointed out tiredly. 'Winning Grands Prix should no longer be a problem for me; my aim next year must be the world championship.'

Any decision about his plans became even more acute in Canada, when Alan Rees tempted Jochen with what was probably the highest offer ever made to a racing driver: £100,000 if he signed for March. Jochen was tempted to accept, particularly as Robin Herd had designed the car. He probably would have signed if Rees had already secured the money.

Brabham, not usually the most loquacious of people, was talking actively in terms of Jochen's return to his team: 'We believed everything was fixed. What finally decided Jochen in favour of Lotus was Chapman's supplementary offer of a Formula 2 team. Jochen liked Formula 2 and the idea of having his own team. That was how we lost him.' Chapman was convinced that a top driver was bound to be better off with Lotus because the sponsors would recognise

Jochen Rindt

his record of success. Asked in Canada if it wasn't sheer madness to pay so much for 'that Rindt', he replied: 'What am I to do? Stewart has pushed up the prices.' Jochen asked Bernie Ecclestone to fly over to Canada to handle the negotiations. He left his options open: 'We must give Brabham another twenty-four hours.' As before, if Brabham could only reach two-thirds of the Lotus offer, Jochen would rejoin him. Desperate conferences followed, with Bernie bringing Goodyear in, but Jack had to concede: 'Sorry, but I cannot raise the money and we'd like to make some money rather than lose it.'

Thus, just before the US Grand Prix at Watkins Glen, Jochen signed the Lotus contract for 1970, which contained a special clause: should Jochen win the championship, he would place himself at the disposal of Lotus for six months of publicity and promotion. He never discussed the March again with Robin Herd, and Alan Rees never mentioned it.

CHAPTER EIGHTEEN

Watkins Glen: Jochen at Last

It was a typical episode in Jochen's career: on the same day that he finally declined Jack's offer, the Brabhams finished one-two in the Canadian Grand Prix, with Jochen coming in third behind Ickx and Brabham. Just before the American Grand Prix, Lotus racing manager Andrew Ferguson sent Jochen a letter in which he set out the somewhat complicated prize money system at Watkins Glen. To give him an example, Ferguson pre-supposed a third place. Jochen flew off in a happy frame of mind.

At night, seen from the air, New York looks like a black velvet cushion in which some lights sparkle like rubies and others shine like sapphires. The helicopter between John F Kennedy and La Guardia Airports takes only four minutes. Another 55 minutes by Mohawk 1-11 takes you to Elmira. Somehow this town sounds like Peter Cheyney and Lemmy Caution; in fact, it is the birthplace of Mark Twain and Tom Sawyer.

Watkins Glen is twenty minutes away by car. It has the forgotten air of an abandoned gold diggers' town. The surroundings are distinctly Austrian—mountains and lots of small lakes—but it is much too cold to bathe in Lake Seneca and the swimming pool at the Glen Motor Inn is unheated.

The entire Grand Prix family puts up in this motel. Victor, the owner, occasionally drives an old McLaren in Can-Am races; his wife is on christian name terms with all the Grand Prix drivers. The lobby is filled with hundreds of racing photographs and in the bar you can't move. It's the experts who come here: 'The informed people'.

The Glen National Bank looks after the enormous prize money—the winner alone gets $50,000. On the Monday morning after the race team managers queue to cash their cheques and the 'Grand Prix Corporation' counts its receipts. Admission tickets cost $10 each; many fans rent trucks and come in groups, sitting on crates of beer.

During practice days the sheriffs literally battle with the crowds trying to get into the 'Techcenter': that's where the racing cars are serviced, for at Watkins Glen, as at Indianapolis, there is no paddock in the European sense. The reactions of the spectators are always the same. During practice they take an equal interest in cars and drivers; after final practice they only look at the cars, and after the race there is nothing but the drivers—the cars are sometimes damaged without regard.

Jochen captured pole position for the fifth time in 1969 and for the seventh time ever, and this alone was worth $2,000. He revealed himself as self-possessed and not over-excited during these days at Watkins Glen: a man sure of things, who feels it's going to be a good weekend.

It was just like Silverstone all over again during the opening laps; Rindt led up to lap 11, and Stewart from then until lap 20, but from then on it was only Rindt. Once Jochen lost four seconds lapping slower cars and Stewart closed up on him, but then Jochen pulled away and on the 35th lap he had the satisfaction of seeing a pit signal: STEW OUT. With Jackie's damaged engine there disappeared his dream of $50,000.

It was a lonely race for Jochen. Behind him Piers Courage was keeping the two works Brabhams at bay. However much they changed their tactics, both of them attacking alternately, Piers stayed in front so successfully that he received the 'man of the race' award.

At the beginning of the final lap Jochen had a lead of 40

Watkins Glen: Jochen at Last

seconds over Courage. This time there was no wing failure, no knuckle joint failure, no shortage of petrol and no Beltoise in the way — only Tex Hopkins, leaping in the air and flailing his chequered flag.

Jochen was astounded: 'There was no overpowering feeling of happiness, perhaps because I should have won so often in the past. Until the last moment I didn't believe the car would last. Not till the final lap, and not quite even then.' It took Jochen 48 Grands Prix to do what Stewart had done in eight and Ickx in seven — and what Regazzoni subsequently did in five and Fittipaldi in four. It remained a puzzle to him, too. As always Chapman dashed into the middle of the track and threw his cap up in the air before the second man had even come into sight.

The second man was Courage, the Old Etonian with his typically English features. Reluctant to take advantage of his background or to live on other people's money, he chose independence. He himself was not wealthy, and Sally was not as rich as most people thought. Courage wanted success but didn't worry about fame; the ambitions came from Sally and from Frank Williams. Sally would have liked him to be world champion, and that would have made Frank rich too.

Motor racing changed Piers and left its mark: rushing over to his friend to offer his congratulations, his face wore what Williams called 'a Worldwide Smile'.

As second man home Courage earned $20,000; Rindt shared his winner's $50,000 with the team and the same applied to his bonus payments: £1,000 from Ford, £1,000 from Shell, £2,450 from Firestone, £50 from Hepolite, £60 from Ferodo, £40 from Automotive Products, £100 from Lucas and £400 from Autolite. The standard recompense for a Grand Prix winner. Jochen felt on top of the world.

But the victory celebration was more subdued at Elmira hospital by the bedside of a seriously injured Graham Hill, 'which rather sobered up the occasion'. Nina had stayed at home because of the travel expenses, and so had Sally. The clover leaf was not complete.

While neither Jochen nor Piers would have made a special trip to visit each other, their friendship had steadily grown; the wives, too, got on well together. To Williams the relationship was 'almost too perfect'.

CHAPTER NINETEEN
Show Time

'A thousand congratulations on your wonderful win! I'm delighted that finally we have been able to give you that which your efforts deserve,' Andrew Ferguson wrote to Jochen. Moss felicitated him on his 'fantastic drive'. He had seen many Grands Prix, but reckoned Watkins Glen equalled any of them.

Jochen finished fourth in the 1969 world championship table with 22 points behind Stewart (63), Ickx (37) and McLaren (26), but he had neither the time nor the inclination to rest on his American laurels; put bluntly, Formula 1 was not for Jochen Rindt the most important part of his life. 'First came his Show, because that was his own personal creation, then his Formula 2 team, of which he was very proud, and then his world championship ambitions.' This is how Bernie Ecclestone saw it, and Bernie had helped him to build up his Formula 2 team.

Jochen once described Bernie by saying: 'He only needs to walk through a showroom and give each car the briefest glance to tell you their total value, having worked it all out in his head. Roy Salvadori, who is also a car dealer, can do the same, but he needs a whole day and masses of paper.'

The name *Jochen Rindt Racing* used to appear in Formula 3 race programmes because Jochen lent his name—and his Austrian entrant's licence—to Frank Williams in the days when Frank used to be a driver. 'That way I used to get more starting money,' Frank recalled, 'but Jochen never asked me

Jochen Rindt

for anything nor did he get anything.' Jochen built up his Formula 2 team on a businesslike basis. 'Could you devote half an hour of your time every day to manage my Formula 2 team?' Jochen asked Bernie. Bernie accepted, never realising that during 1970 he would be devoting half an hour to his dealership and $23\frac{1}{2}$ hours to the team that he and Jochen ran on a fifty/fifty basis.

Bernie never went up to Hethel for his negotiations with Chapman, 'because Chapman is always too busy at the factory.' Instead Chapman flew down to Biggin Hill in his Navajo, complete with secretary; Bernie drove over in seven minutes from his Bexleyheath car emporium. The conference took place on board the plane. If it was foggy, Chapman arrived by car. Bernie found time to attend only a few of the 1970 Formula 2 races; had he been present, he would have been proud to see how Jochen ran the team. 'I am my own Mark McCormack,' Jochen often used to say when talk turned to Stewart's five-year contract with the American promotions outfit. 'I manage myself.'

This certainly applied to the Jochen Rindt Show. Jochen created this racing car exhibition in Vienna in 1965, investing £10,000; before long no major company could afford not to take part. Jochen signed five-year contracts with the British Formula 1 teams, organised convoys of transporters to bring the cars over, arranged for racing films to be shown, dealt with correspondence and phone calls, and sold the Show in places as diverse as Munich, Essen and Belgrade. He was well on the way to acquiring all the European rights; jokingly he told his assistant Udo Poschmann: 'Why don't we rent a Jumbo jet and sell the admission tickets at the foot of the steps; it'll save us transport costs as well as hiring a hall.' In 1969 he ran the Show in spite of feverish flu and later suffered from gastritis, which was the result of overwork rather than of racing.

Jochen had to make his apologies for the traditional Lotus Dinner Dance at London's Europe Hotel; he couldn't get

Show Time

away from the Show. Consequently he received a letter from the Lotus PR man, asking him to mark the 1970 dinner-dance date in his diary so as to avoid letting the Rindt Show and other things clash with it. Chapman installed a phone hook-up and loudspeaker so as to bring his guests a live conversation between Rindt and Hill. Graham was still lying in a London hospital and was being treated with heroin because morphia wasn't strong enough. Jochen made one of the nicest remarks I heard in 1969: 'Pity you can't be here in Vienna to open the Show for me, but I can't afford you, Graham.' Loud laughter drowned Hill's reply.

'Actually, I've never tried to economise on my Show,' Jochen once told me. Hoping to achieve the world championship crown in order to save the expense of having to import another world champion, he didn't hesitate to bring over the 'fastest man in the world', Art Arfons and his 'Green Monster' from America; on another occasion Juan Manuel Fangio came over from Argentina. Jackie Stewart applauded 'the second Jochen Rindt Show I have seen; the first one was at Watkins Glen!' Just before the formal opening in 1969 Jackie asked Jochen what he should do. Jochen replied: 'Just hang around.' Jackie grinned in return. 'When I arrived at the airport, somebody said: "That must be a friend of Jochen."'

Jochen organised Rolls-Royce hire cars and opera tickets for his prominent guests. He was heart, brain and muscle all in one. 'An outstanding ambassador for Austria,' as Hill once observed. Only rarely did Jochen drop a remark which showed how proud he really was of his Show. It was to be the basis of his post-racing life. Even now it is the biggest in Europe. On no other occasion away from the Grand Prix tracks were the elite of motor racing so well represented as at Vienna in 1969.

Leo Mehl and Bob Martin, the Goodyear and Firestone racing bosses, were present, as was the most important of them all, Ford Vice President Walter Hayes.

Jochen Rindt

'If I weren't interested to see Rindt as the 1970 world champion, I wouldn't be here,' Hayes told me. 'It would be a wonderful thing for our sport to have a German-speaking champion.' Which meant in other words that Hayes would do everything possible to help Rindt get his title.

Admittedly some drivers spread a story of Cosworth changing numbers round and sending back different engines after servicing, but Hayes insists: 'Ford powers Formula 1, but doesn't try to influence it. And I only intervene when things go wrong. Incidentally I helped Jochen on several occasions in 1969 without mentioning it.'

Hayes told me the only time he interfered actively in any race was at Watkins Glen in 1967. 'The world championship was already out of reach for Lotus, Clark, Hill and Ford, but we all knew just what the American Grand Prix meant for every one of us. I wanted a one-two victory; above all I wanted to avoid a dice between two Ford drivers. The evening before the Grand Prix we tossed for it at Chapman's suggestion. Hill won and Clark was in agreement.' Graham and Jimmy drove according to instructions. But Hill's engine started spluttering and Amon's Ferrari was getting closer. Clark made desperate hand signals, asking for instructions. Hayes conferred with Chapman. 'Move ahead for a win!' Jimmy was told. Then Amon dropped out and Hill's engine picked up again . . . but Clark still won in spite of a rear wheel which all but came off on the last lap!

'Sorry, Graham, I didn't cheat, I obeyed pit orders,' Clark apologised. 'Never mind,' Hill grunted. If this gives an indication of the chivalry of the sport it also exposes the problem of driving to team orders. Hayes never did it again, and Hill later phoned him to ask if he might tell the story in his book. 'Of course,' Hayes said. 'It's a beautiful story.'

Ford had built 42 Formula 1 power units by the end of 1969; another 25 were planned for 1970. 'Last year cost us £230,000; just a quarter of Porsche's race budget.' The drivers would assume more importance than ever before, forecast

Show Time

Hayes and prophesied the coming world championship position, which was to prove entirely accurate up to third place at two stages of the game: 'First Rindt, because he deserves the title; second Brabham, the only one whose new car will be completely sorted out at the beginning of the season; and third Stewart, because Tyrrell is doing a great deal of work on his March; fourth Ickx, but only if he stays absolute number one at Ferrari, for he thrives on this sort of responsibility; fifth Siffert, who has been under-rated for too long; and sixth either McLaren, who is devoting too much of his time to his Can-Am cars, or Courage, because the de Tomaso is still an unknown quantity.' Hayes also foresaw the arrival in Formula 1 of the 22-year-old Brazilian Fittipaldi and said it would not surprise him if Fittipaldi became world champion before Ickx achieved it.

Comparing Rindt and Stewart, Hayes thought Jackie was the 'more clearly thinking driver', but Jochen 'the absolute fastest'.

Winter flies, what with ski-ing holidays in Zürs, where Courage 'skis like a girl' according to Jochen, and with tyre testing at Kyalami in South Africa. Racing teams are paid £2 to £3 per mile to test new tyres, for even the biggest of manufacturers need practical experience to develop their products. And Firestone had to catch up on the enormous lead Goodyear had acquired over the past few months. During 600 laps of testing, John Miles wore out four engines, Jochen only one. . . . Jochen also visited Keith Duckworth, who had left Lotus in 1960.

The maximum revs of the Ford engines had been limited in 1969 by an automatic governor working on centrifugal principles. For 1970 this limiter was to be adjustable, and Lucas had produced a new governor which was linked to the ignition system and worked on impulses. While this set a normal maximum of 10,200 rpm, the driver was able to over-ride it with a switch so that a few extra revs were available temporarily for overtaking. The McLarens were the first to

Jochen Rindt

receive this equipment in 1970. Chapman later connected a very thin wire to this switch, which broke as soon as the switch was flicked: 'I don't want to see my £7,500 engines over-revved by the drivers.' Rindt was never to make use of his rev limit eliminator in 1970, and Miles utilised it only once, in practice at Hockenheim.

At the big annual Lotus press conference in London on February 25th, Chapman officially announced his decision neither to enter for Indianapolis nor for the Can-Am series, but to concentrate on the main objective, the Formula 1 world championship. Sports Minister Denis Howell received a model of a Lotus 49; Tony Garrett, chairman of Player's, was given Jochen's Watkins Glen steering wheel.

As a result of this cut-back six Indy and seven GT mechanics had to leave the racing department, and Dick Scammell had to pick the very best for the Formula 1 team; Gordon Huckle became chief mechanic, and Jochen's car was entrusted to 32-year-old Eddie Dennis and 21-year-old Mike 'Herbie' Blash, a farmer's son who formerly worked for Rob Walker and is a Manchester United football fan. Both of them adored Jochen. 'He was a little moody, but we got to know when to talk to him and when to shut up.' Eddie's wedding anniversary is September 5th, something he forgot every year for ten years, but he's never likely to forget it again after 1970.

CHAPTER TWENTY

Kyalami: Imperfect Paradise

Half-way between Johannesburg—the 80-year-old gold mining town—and Pretoria—the capital—is the Kyalami Ranch, a bungalow-type hotel with a swimming pool. Jochen once described it as a 'dream paradise, if only it were managed better'. As both air crews and racing drivers have their habitual rooms, and as in the best South African manner no-one ever wants to say 'no', double bookings occur during the Grand Prix Circus and some guests have to change rooms. The most frequent migrant during our week at Kyalami seemed to be Jacky Ickx, constantly following a black porter with his luggage.

The hills are flat-topped, the eucalyptus trees on top appear like ants. Everywhere there is the scent of the pale pink national flower, the proteas. The hum of the air-conditioning mixes with the loudspeaker music, the splashing of the fountain and the almost excessive twitter of the birds. In the afternoons they fly over the ranch in vee formation, reminiscent of the Matra and BRM 12-cylinder engines; in the evenings it is easy to find the Southern Cross in the dark sky.

Life by the pool is easy. Ickx roasts in the sun from 8 am onwards. Stewart has gained some extra weight during the winter—just like his March, which has a 180-pound surplus—and worries that he feels hungry again an hour after the safari breakfast. Servoz-Gavin is thrown out of the breakfast room because he is only wearing Bermuda shorts, and goes

Jochen Rindt

off for a game of tennis with Jackie. Andretti wets himself three times before finally jumping into the pool. The wind occasionally carries high-pitched engine noises from the track where people are practising—most of all Hill, who in spite of his bad limp is hoping for an unexpectedly early come-back.

Rob Walker, Graham's new boss, is in his safari outfit and looks exactly like the real Stanley out of the history book; Ken Tyrrell, with his large bony features, looks more like a gold-digger.

On Tuesday, at around half-past five, Andretti went off the road in the STP-March and smashed into a wooden post. 'The rear brakes locked,' I said to Rindt, who arrived dead tired after flying right through the night. 'Mario doesn't need any excuses,' Jochen answered. 'I only hope I won't be in the vicinity when any of the Marches go off.'

Short of sleep, Jochen's best time on Wednesday was 1 minute 20.1 seconds, the same as Hulme's. 'Just to look at Denny gives me a headache,' Jochen said. 'He is as strong as an ox, particularly in this heat. Everyone here has their problems of course. Stewart, for instance: he can't get under 1 minute 21 seconds because of the Dunlops.'

Jochen, too, had a tyre problem. In spite of 600 test laps, in spite of all the claims made for them, the new Firestones ran much too hot; they vibrated, and they gave the drivers the impression they were driving on oil.

Chapman slept badly that night. The mosquitoes bothered him and the insecticide couldn't be found; when the telephonist finally rang him back with this information she said she hoped he wouldn't be bitten to death. He spent the morning by the pool, in borrowed swimming trunks, reading Puzo's *The Godfather,* about the Mafia. John Miles, who looks like a theology student, dozed beside him. Jochen remarked to Stewart: 'I had a look at your house a few days ago. The new chimney looks good.' Jackie nodded. 'Are we having a big press party at Begnins again next week during the

Natascha's second birthday

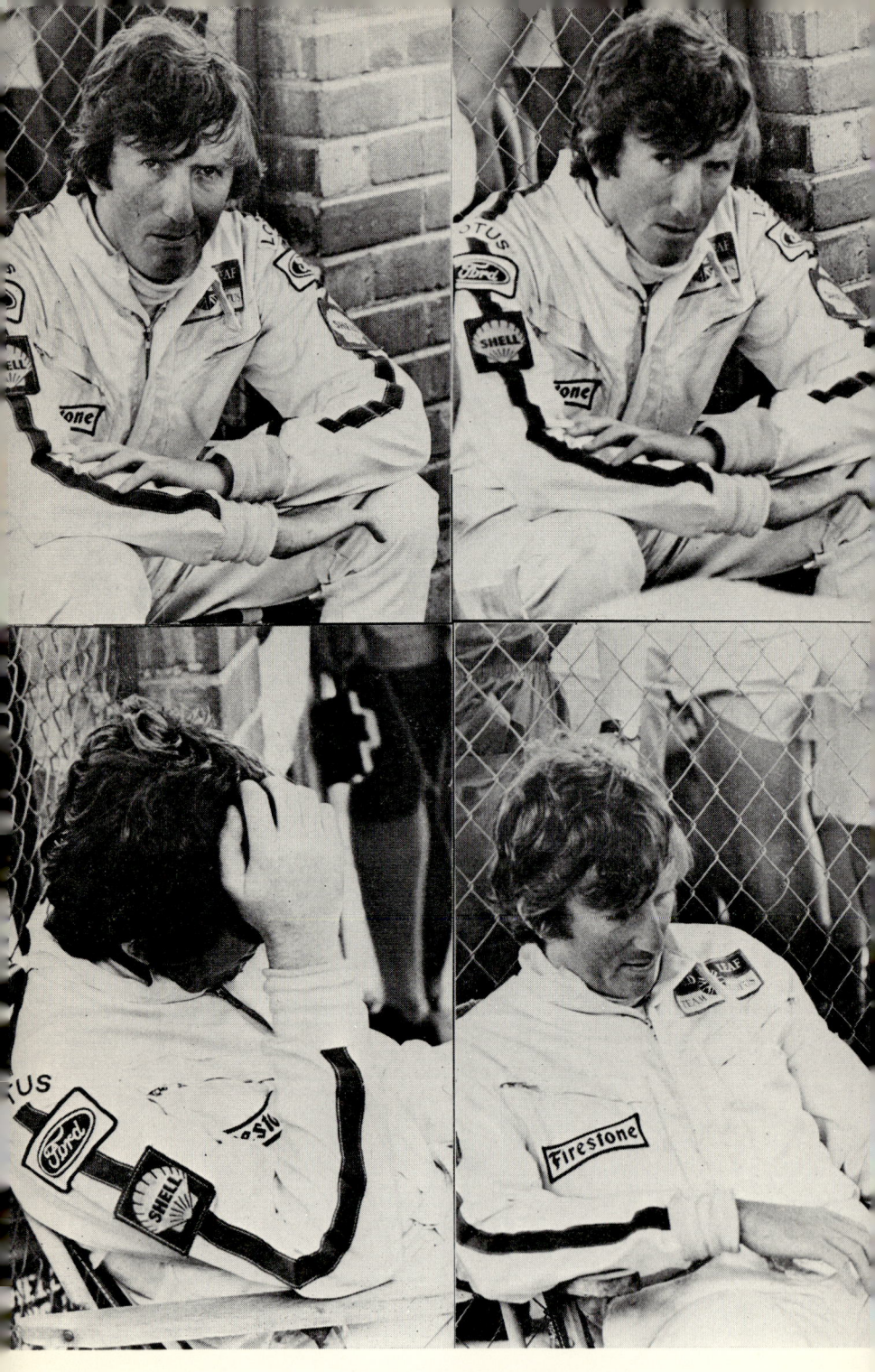

Waiting in the paddock

Kyalami: Imperfect Paradise

Geneva Show?' Jochen said he would have to carry half the cost and suddenly looked thoughtful.

Jochen phoned Nina that evening because it was their third wedding anniversary. 'My wife would have liked to join us,' said Dick Scammell afterwards, 'but it gets too expensive.' Jochen grinned the way he often did when talking about money, and rattled off: '£268 10s 6d from Geneva.'

In the afternoon, while Jochen busied himself in the pits, Stewart and Amon managed the identical 1 minute 19.3 seconds which gained them (and March) the best two starting positions.

During practice, while he was showing Stommelen the way round, Jack Brabham's right rear tyre came off the rim; it was found to have been badly mounted. 'I think they are pushing things to the limit as far as tyres are concerned,' Rindt observed to Chapman.

During the final session, as if on command, every single March — Stewart, Servoz-Gavin, Amon, Siffert and Andretti — suddenly appeared on the circuit in close formation like a jet fighter squadron. How March had managed to finance the construction of five cars was still a mystery to Jochen. By fitting higher gear ratios he managed fastest lap that day, but still only made the second row of the grid.

On race day I had breakfast with Jochen: 'The big question is how fast each driver decides to go. I think I'll hang back and bide my time. The one to watch will be Amon.' Under the sunshade, Rindt and Chapman were giving former four-wheel-drive guinea-pig Miles starting tips for his first two-wheel drive Formula 1 race. 'First gear almost up to 10,000, then second gear until you hear the rev limiter,' Jochen advised.

In the South African Grand Prix Jochen only got as far as the first bend without incident. 'I was lying third and following the ideal line for the corner when I was suddenly rammed from behind by Brabham. The Lotus leapt six feet into the air, landed on its left wheels and slid off onto the

Jochen Rindt

grass.' All Stewart could see in his mirror was a cloud of dust; Siffert and Ickx saw 'an enormous jumble of wheels'.

The engine died on Jochen, but as he was still moving he slammed the gearlever into first and accelerated away; by the time the pack passed the pits for the first time he had already retaken Andretti, Hill, Courage, Love, Eaton and de Klerk. Two places behind came Amon, who pit-stopped after ten laps and swore bitterly about 'bloody Rindt'. 'The shunt should never have happened; I was afraid Rindt would turn over.'

Out in front, Brabham caught Stewart after nineteen laps, and Hulme followed him through shortly afterwards. So from lap 38 onwards two Goodyear drivers headed Jackie, who was unable to make any impression in spite of some spirited ten-tenths driving. Jochen battled on with a bent rear wishbone: 15th on lap 5, 14th on lap 6, 13th on lap 7, 10th on lap 8, 9th on lap 13, 8th on lap 40, 7th by lap 54, 6th by lap 59 and 5th from lap 60 onwards. As the amount of oil and rubber on the track increased, the tyres were gripping less and less. And eight laps from the end his engine failed, so all the effort had been for nothing.

'Tell Miles place 5,' Chapman ordered, not realising that John had been sitting in a pool of petrol ever since the third lap, thanks to a split tank. 'If I'd been you, I would have pit-stopped,' Jochen said afterwards. 'That stuff goes up too damned easily.'

Brabham thus won his first Grand Prix since Canada 1967; the band played *Waltzing Matilda* and he drank champagne. Jochen stepped over to Ron Tauranac: 'Jack bumped me.' Ron smiled and suggested that Jack thought the opposite. In the end, neither blamed the other; they both believed it was Andretti's fault, though Mario wasn't even near enough to see the incident. Could it be the red car they both saw was Amon's?

Immediately after the race a downpour commenced. 30,000 cars were stuck helplessly in the mud. Stewart was offered

Kyalami: Imperfect Paradise

the help of a plump blonde, who gave him a lift back to the Ranch on her motorbike; Jochen, Miles and I braved the thunderstorm on foot.

Chapman, who had left his rented car some way down the road, had already taken off from the airport. Over steak and melons, his team analysed the tyre drama. They all noticed how Ickx and Surtees, both on Firestone, had speeded up or slowed down at exactly the same time. 'I'll have to ring Firestone,' Jochen decided, 'because at the moment I'm pretty unhappy with the tyres and we'll have to do some more testing. The tyre advantage is with Brabham at the moment, but then Jack and his cars are always hot competition.'

Stewart categorised the fresh developments at Kyalami for me as follows: 'The Brabham looks extremely healthy; the McLaren very workmanlike; BRM obviously have a good chassis; and the Matra is probably the best chassis of all; the Ferrari's handling is first class too. We can only pin our hopes on reliability once the new Lotus makes its appearance.'

The new Lotus, already described by Hayes as 'very exciting', was Chapman's greatest pride, at least since he introduced the Lotus 25 monocoque in which Jim Clark became the first 'horizontal' driver. 'A bed on wheels' was the way Clark had described it.

CHAPTER TWENTY-ONE

Lotus 72

Maurice Phillippe has a crafty smile about him; drops the odd word of German here and there; looks—if anything—like a bookkeeper, and never loses his pale British complexion no matter how hot the sun. He was responsible, under Chapman's supervision, for the design of the Lotus 72, commenced in the middle of November 1969.

By re-locating the various components of the car, better weight distribution resulted. The radiator was split and moved to either side of the cockpit, avoiding pipes passing through it as well as excessive heat around the driver—and incidentally reducing frontal area. The rubber fuel tanks held 48 gallons. Fuel melodramas like Clark's at Monza (1967) and Rindt's at Silverstone (1969) were to be eliminated by building a much simpler fuel feed system, 'the best we ever had', for it would work with as little as one-fifth of a gallon in the tank.

The suspension was based on torsion bars. And the front brakes were located inboard, resulting in a considerable reduction in unsprung weight, but adding to technical complexities. As all conventional Grand Prix cars had their front brakes attached directly to the stub axle, an additional link had to be included between the wheel and brake disc: this was achieved by means of a double universally-jointed driveshaft.

'At first, Jochen was not exactly enamoured by this idea, but I was able to convince him as to the car's inherent safety

Lotus 72

and the advantages offered by those inboard brakes,' Chapman reported. 'Tens of thousands of family saloons—Citroens are one example—use such a system. Thus I can't be considered entirely original.'

No less than 84 companies supplied components for the new Lotus. The laid-down minimum weight for Formula 1 cars is 530 kgs, of which 30 is intended for safety equipment like roll bar, fire extinguisher and seat harness. 'We are less close to the limit than people seem to believe,' Chapman added. 'According to Ron Tauranac, the new Brabham is eight kilograms over the minimum, and that corresponds closely with ours.'

Rindt had to work hard for his five 1969 pole positions in the Lotus 49; in the Lotus 72 he could be more relaxed, he would not have to exhaust himself. The engine's 425 bhp would be transferred more efficiently onto the road, thanks to the weight distribution of 70 per cent on the rear wheels.

'If the car runs as well as it looks, it's going to be sensational,' was Jochen's first impression, but 'we didn't do enough testing'. For this reason, a problem which should have been discovered under really intensive testing was not actually revealed until the car reached the extreme heat of the Spanish Grand Prix; the twenty-lap trial carried out beforehand by Jochen at Snetterton unfortunately took place in wet conditions.

CHAPTER TWENTY-TWO

Jarama: the Shorn Lotus Blossom

Looking rather like a bloated star-fish, the 2-mile long Jarama circuit lies thirteen parched miles north of Madrid, totally exposed to the glare of the sun. Although it was only the middle of April, the surrounding *piscinas* or swimming pools were already in use. Jarama Park is a green oasis in a barren landscape; the Spanish Automobile Club has converted 90 per cent of it into a golf course and 10 per cent into a race track.

With two second-gear hairpins and four third-gear corners, Jochen considered Jarama a Mickey Mouse course, but found it more strenuous than Monte Carlo.

1.35 pm on the Thursday: not many cars had arrived as yet. Three Lotus 49s, two works cars and the one belonging to Rob Walker, were still being held by Spanish Customs at the frontier. Graham Hill was not amused: 'They can't consider an old Lotus like that valuable?'

Rindt had done just ten laps in the Lotus 72. 'We have a few small problems, but then the 72 is such a new animal,' commented Maurice Phillippe, the car's designer. While Jochen sat in the cockpit someone passed him a sandwich. 'Give it to Colin,' he mouthed through his Nomex mask; he wanted to be off again.

Only later on did an investigation reveal what was happening while Jochen sat in his car. It is common knowledge that the energy of a moving car is converted into friction, i.e. heat, as soon as the brakes are applied. To prevent the

Jarama: the Shorn Lotus Blossom

transfer of heat to the universal joints when the car stops, an insulating spacer was built in between these joints and the brake discs. In conventional designs with outboard brakes, this heat ($500°$-$600°F$) is dissipated into the wheels and hubs. But with the inboard brakes of the Lotus 72 this is no longer possible, so the heat flow is reduced by insulating material.

'We used the same insulating material in 1969 on the Indy cars,' Eddie, one of the mechanics, recalled. 'But that wasn't much of a problem because you hardly need to brake at Indy.' In any case the air flow at speed kept the temperature constant. But at Jarama the heat which built up while Jochen was waiting in the pits was transmitted.

First lap 1 minute 30.8 seconds; second lap 1 minute 27.4 seconds; third lap 1 minute 28.6 seconds; fourth lap 1 minute 29.0 seconds, according to Chapman's stop watch.

Fifth lap: at the braking point, 120 yards from the end of the 800-yard long finishing straight, just before the third-gear right-hander, Jochen stepped on the brake pedal. At that moment the bolts holding the left brake disc snapped.

'The car was thrown over to the right immediately; I spun twice into the infield, back onto the track and luckily came to rest just eighteen inches from the fence,' Jochen reported later. Stewart saw the dust cloud, jumped onto the wall and called out to Chapman: 'That was Jochen, he's stopped, but he's OK. He's pushing the car.' Jackie dropped back onto the track to warn the approaching Brabham, but Black Jack turned off into the pit road. Chapman and the mechanics jumped into the nearest car and chased over to the corner.

I gave them a hand with the car. Jochen was not pleased. 'That's a fine start. I was fantastically lucky: I couldn't have got off more lightly.' The Lotus 72 smelled of hot rubber; pebbles and bits of paper stuck to the oily tyres and there hung around a faint odour of carbolic acid. The shorn Lotus Blossom was pushed into its garage and the wooden shutters closed, to the disappointment of the curious bystanders. 'The shop's closed for today,' Jochen told them. Stewart came to have a look through the back door, but Chapman mumbled: 'Would you excuse us, please,' whereupon Jackie shrugged his shoulders and wandered away.

None of the Lotus boys got any sleep that night, but the car was ready for practice on Friday morning. 'That Lotus is going to be very, very good, but we should have done some more testing,' Jochen told me. Did he regard the defect as a 'symptom of youth' or as a serious problem, I asked him. Jochen looked at me but remained silent. Only later did he tell me, trying to sound casual: 'It's pretty clear to me that something will go wrong. That's why I'm quite pleased to be driving here because this track is relatively safe.' The lap average is pretty low, about 90 mph.

Two things had been done to the 72. The insulating material had been replaced by a steel spacer, and ventilated discs had been fitted in place of the original solid ones. In addition Jochen was instructed to complete a slow lap before each pit stop in order to give the discs a chance to cool down. Chapman later blamed Jochen for Thursday's incident, because he claimed to have mentioned this precautionary procedure earlier: Jochen didn't accept this.

Late on Friday evening, while Phillippe and Scammell dined with their wives, Jochen (in lilac velvet suit) and Nina (in maxi-skirt and boots) were joined by Courage in the lobby of the 'Luz Palacio' in the Paseo de la Castellana. 'I'm only using four gears,' Jochen stated. 'Do you drive over the kerbs?' Piers wanted to know. Jochen didn't. Piers talked about the de Tomaso which 'oversteered like a pig'; admittedly he had never seen a pig which oversteered, 'but you understand what I mean.' Jochen grinned and Piers had another complaint. 'Going up to that corner on top of the hill in fourth, I was heading directly into the sun and I couldn't see anything.'

On Saturday, during qualification trials, the de Tomaso hit the guard rail at precisely this point. It bounced back and impaled itself on a wooden post. Piers returned on foot. 'I

Jarama: the Shorn Lotus Blossom

only saw your second impact,' Stewart told him, 'but even that was pretty spectacular.' Jochen and Nina rushed over: 'Did anything break?' Jochen asked suspiciously. Piers shook his head; I asked him if it could have been oil. 'I hope so, otherwise I have no excuse at all; the car suddenly became so light.'

Jochen was using 14½-inch wide rear tyres, the same which Porsche fitted towards the end of 1969 on their 'white monsters', and like Stewart and Amon he had a new Ford engine. To celebrate his 28th birthday, Jochen munched a birthday cake which had been given to him by the BBC *Wheelbase* crew. While the fight to qualify for the last five places on the grid was under way, the loudspeaker played romantic Spanish airs. In spite of the efforts of flamboyantly dressed racing director Conte de Villapadierna, who tried to help everybody, there was chaos. The organisers could not even make up their minds how many cars would be allowed to start. 'Why don't you give Soler-Roig pole position?' Lotus competitions manager Andrew Ferguson generously suggested to one of the harassed officials.

The arguments about qualifying and the starting grid continued into the night. Eventually it was agreed that twenty cars would start, but then it was pointed out that this contravened the supplementary regulations for the race. Siffert was dragged out of his car on the start line; the police waded into everyone with their truncheons, so Miles and Soler-Roig pushed their cars away voluntarily. Hill dropped an acid remark, whereupon the police tried to drag him out of his cockpit too, 'because of rude behaviour'. Graham, secure in his car with his harness fastened, kept quiet but his moustache bristled. Originally they gave Jochen only thirteenth best practice time; then Lotus 'did something about it' and he finished in the third row with Ickx and Amon, in front of Oliver. Even during the warming-up lap Jochen's new engine only fired cleanly between 9,500 and 10,000 rpm. Lynn, Oliver's dark-haired bride, who used to be a sales repre-

Jochen Rindt

sentative for Gold Leaf, busied herself handing out free stickers issued by BRM's new £45,000 sponsors: Yardley, the cosmetics firm.

On the first lap, rushing down to one of the second-gear hairpins, Oliver's BRM suffered front hub failure, slithered over the grass and torpedoed Ickx's Ferrari amidships, as the closely following Rindt was to put it later.

Within a second and a half the Ferrari became engulfed in flames leaping twenty feet into the air; an amateur film camera recorded the flames as they spread to the BRM, and within nine seconds the fire-fighters were on the scene. Oliver released his seat-belt buckle, leapt out of his car and stumbled towards the pits, unharmed save for singed eyebrows. Ickx was trapped in his squashed cockpit, due to the side impact it received; he could hardly move, and according to his estimate it took him fifteen to twenty seconds to undo the straps and escape. When he finally got out of the car he fell into the blazing petrol which was running across the road, and had to roll on the grass to put out the flames. McLaren, Rindt, Hill and the rest, slowed their cars to a walking pace and managed to avoid the gruesome area of explosions, conflagration and black smoke clouds by taking to the grass. 'Within fractions of a second the whole track was alight, but not badly enough to obscure the wrecked cars.'

The foam and water used by the fire-fighters formed a greasy, soapy surface. Unexpectedly, the burning Ferrari started rolling back towards McLaren, who only just managed to avoid it. The westerly wind drove the black smoke over the pit straight, and everyone was in the grip of cold, naked fear. After ten laps, Rindt, who had been lying seventh behind Stewart, Hulme, Brabham, Beltoise, Pescarolo and McLaren, went missing. Nina was about to rush off to find him when Jochen arrived on foot: 'Engine trouble. But I'm OK. Who's leading?' 'Stewart,' Chapman said pensively.

Brabham decided to have a go at Stewart from lap 50 onwards, but eleven laps later he was forced to retire when

Jarama: the Shorn Lotus Blossom

his crankshaft broke; Stewart not only led from start to finish but lapped all the surviving runners—McLaren, Andretti, Hill and Servoz-Gavin. He now topped the world championship table with 13 points to Brabham's 9.

Over cold meat and Coca Cola the race dramatics were given an airing in the Gulf caravan. 'I can't understand why they didn't stop the race so as to clear the track,' Jochen remarked to Piers. Louis Stanley warned that the long hair of the present-day generation of drivers presented an additional danger in case of fire. 'That's why he always kept on at Oliver to visit his barber.' Stewart was amused: 'I don't intend to get shorn that way.' McLaren expressed concern whether Ickx had had his face burnt, whereupon Stewart quipped semi-seriously: 'How long are we going to stick to this crazy business, Brucie?'

McLaren didn't intend to continue much longer. His design for a series of road cars, incorporating very up-to-date ideas was all but ready, and he was about to embark on his second major career as an automobile constructor: he had reached the point where his active driving days appeared to be ending.

Ickx was picked up in his future father-in-law's private aircraft to be rushed to Brussels for an operation. Amon finally managed to win his first ever Formula 1 race at Silverstone, but for the Lotus 72 more development was needed.

The suspension was re-designed by Chapman and Phillippe and they completely changed the suspension geometry. 'The new Lotus 72 won't look any different but it will in fact be a completely new car,' Jochen said. Chapman promised its completion by Spa or Zandvoort. This meant that at Monaco Rindt would have to drive the Lotus 49, now four years old; but it had won him his victory at Watkins Glen.

CHAPTER TWENTY-THREE

Monaco, his Biggest Success

Chapman missed the first practice day in Monte Carlo because he and Hazel had tickets for a Frank Sinatra show in London. Jochen turned in fastest practice lap half-way through the first period. On one occasion Miles unintentionally held Jochen up. When they stopped at the pits Jochen pounced on John and asked him: 'Do you know which is the most important part of a racing car for a driver like you?' John appeared puzzled. 'The bloody rear-view mirror,' Jochen snapped. Later his engine packed up.

But the story of the day was written by Rodriguez and Amon: Pedro blocked Amon all the way up to the Casino; Chris finally squeezed by, shaking his fist, but got tangled up with a guard rail, which didn't do the March any good at all. Stommelen, who had an eye-witness view, imagined 'Pedro grinning under his mask'.

Stewart's agency had got for him a Japanese camera worth about £350 for only £100, proving that only the rich know how to save money. Jackie was to be filmed by Roman Polanski, the world-famous producer with the Mickey Mouse face; Kirk Douglas was also in the picture.

As always, Jochen and Bernie Ecclestone soaked up the Monte Carlo atmosphere on board a private yacht; this time it was the ocean-going, £5,000 a month *Crest Cutter*; they invited Chapman to stay with them. Part of this floating hotel's attraction was a 50-horsepower Mercury speedboat; ideal for Jochen to terrorise the shipping around the port.

Monaco, his Biggest Success

On the Thursday before the race Jochen took Bernie's private pilot along for a ride . . . he lost his balance, and broke his leg when he was thrown against one of the seats. 'These fellows just aren't fit enough,' Jochen observed to Ken Tyrrell, another guest for drinks on the *Crest Cutter*.

I stayed in the same hotel as the Lotus mechanics. For the early morning practice on Friday, which started at an unearthly 7.50 (5.40 for the Formula 3 cars) it fell to me to guide them to the Esso garage through the labyrinth of narrow passages and steep steps which are a feature of the Principality. Later I volunteered to get them tea and croissants from the nearest café. These fellows really have a hard job; Eddie Wyss of the McLaren team told me more than once: 'Those Lotus mechanics are the first in the garage and the last to leave; they deserve to win more than anyone else.'

The early morning practice period—hated by the greying playboys and the platinum blondes in their marble retreats of luxury—was rained out. For a long time Brabham, running on rain tyres and with a large umbrella over the open cockpit, was the only one to disturb the peace of the Principality; a one-man show which, one would have thought, was more Jackie Stewart's cup of tea.

Chapman wanted Jochen to go out in the wet, 'because one must drive under adverse conditions to gain experience', but Jochen wasn't in the mood: 'If it rains during the race, that's one thing. But as long as I don't have to, I don't drive in the wet.'

Black rain clouds still hung threateningly over the bay during the afternoon, and high winds stirred up the sea when Jochen decided to take the motor boat out of the harbour. The first officer warned him the sea was much too rough. 'That's exactly why I want to go,' grinned Jochen. Courage and I joined him. 'Piers is an idiot, Piers is an idiot,' Sally Courage mumbled like a gramophone record. 'What's come over him, going with that lunatic Jochen?'

Jochen Rindt

'What am I to tell Frank Williams if you also break your leg?' she shouted. Offended, she retired to her cabin with *The Times* under her arm.

With Jochen and Piers I was to experience fifteen alarming minutes of flat-out speedboating; far more thrilling than some high-speed laps with Jochen in a 3-litre prototype. Jochen passed his seamanship test in 1969 after only two hours' instruction and was hunched over the steering wheel with a fierce grin. The poor motor boat practically burst its seams. The 'yumping' from wave to wave really hurt, and I was sitting in the bow on the seat where the pilot broke his leg!

Soaked to the skin and tasting salt we returned to port. Piers looked at his watch: '4.20 — tea time.' Later on Jochen took another trip and related: 'At one time the boat rose up vertically; I really thought we would capsize. I wouldn't have given a fag for our chances.' After dinner in the Pirate Club Jochen felt ill, and during the night he was overcome by seasickness on the pitching *Crest Cutter*. His Alka Seltzer cure being ineffective, his green face even greener in contrast to his brown cowboy jacket, he dragged himself across the harbour for the final practice session, climbed over the guard rail and found relief under a tree. During the Formula 3 race Helmut Marko crashed his McNamara at the Tobacconist's when a drive-shaft broke. 'This is one place where I don't need to worry too much, because the Lotus 49 is built quite well,' Jochen growled.

The sea was still rough that afternoon, and waves were breaking over the wall near the Portier: 'Coping with the spray needed a lot of concentration and was tiring; I'm glad I didn't have to qualify,' Jochen said. Servoz-Gavin's Tyrrell-March made violent contact with the chicane, and Graham Hill's Lotus crashed on the way up to the Casino. As Miles's Lotus 49 had failed to qualify, it was loaned to Graham and repainted in the midnight blue of the Rob Walker team. 'Tomorrow evening,' cursed the Lotus mechanics, 'we'll have to scrape the whole lot off again.'

Monaco, his Biggest Success

Stewart was on pole position with Amon alongside him; Rindt was next to Pescarolo in the fourth row. A bookmaker had set up his pitch in the Tip Top Bar which is situated on the descent from the Casino to the Mirabeau. Jochen was only rated seventh favourite. The leading odds were Stewart 1:2; Amon 6:4; Hulme 2:1; Brabham 9:4; Siffert 3:1; Courage 3:1; and Rindt 7:2.

Ken Tyrrell, whom I met for a beer at midnight, certainly rated Jochen higher. 'Is Jochen sleeping on his boat again?' he asked, and grinned when I assured him that tonight he would be sleeping excellently.

The lights burned all night in the Esso garage. Chapman, Bernie, Dick and the mechanics were all trying to work out why Jochen was 1.9 seconds slower than Stewart. 'The car isn't set up properly,' Chapman said. 'And Jochen has only been able to use four gears, so we'll have to change the ratios. In addition we're changing the suspension and shock absorber settings and we're putting on new tyres; Jochen will have a completely different car tomorrow.'

It was noon before the sun came out. As always on race day, Jochen tried to sleep as late as possible. 'He used not to be able to, but he's much more relaxed these days,' Nina reflected. Before any race Jochen almost resented direct contact with people; sometimes he didn't even like signing autographs.

Brabham was one of the guests on board for lunch. It was the same old story—Jack and Jochen, almost like brothers. Jochen tempted him to more veal cutlets and salade Niçoise, while Bernie tried to fill up the wine glasses. But Brabham drinks nothing and eats little before a race.

'I'll just go and drive; I know I've got no chance of winning,' Jochen told Nina, but she was less pessimistic: 'Don't be silly, you always have a chance.' Jochen reminded her that he had never got further than the fifty-sixth lap in any Monaco Grand Prix. Bernie Ecclestone pointed out that at Monaco anything can happen. 'You've got to keep going.

Jochen Rindt

Whatever you do don't come into the pits—except on foot!' Bernie feared that if Jochen was not doing well and had problems with the car, he would just give up.

Colin Chapman also felt this concern: 'Look, Jochen, we weren't successful in the first few races but we haven't reached the end of the season yet. There are still eleven races to be won.'

'But not if one is eighth in practice, driving a slow car,' Jochen countered.

'Keep going, don't give up, one doesn't necessarily win a race by leading all the way,' advised Chapman. 'I've seen enough Grand Prix to have learned that lesson.' One of the most surprising things about Jochen, Chapman thought, was that he was either up in the clouds or completely down in the dumps.

Road sweepers had cleaned the 3.14-kilometre circuit immaculately with electric vacuum cleaners. The doors and windows of the 'Hotel de Paris' were barricaded. Prince Rainier, Princess Grace and their children had arrived at their velvet-covered Royal box. The new Clerk of the Course, Paul Frere, had gathered the sixteen drivers together for the briefing, and when he dropped the flag of the Principality he set in motion the 80-lap roulette of Monte Carlo. Stewart once again took the initiative in a race that, by tradition, has never been won by leading all the way. Jackie was driving in 'Jim Clark style' and had opened a gap of 7.5 seconds over his pursuers within ten laps.

Amon, Brabham, Beltoise, Ickx, Hulme, Pescarolo and Rindt formed a colourful chain, pulling away from each other as they flashed by. On lap 12 Ickx's luck ran out; racing even though his Jarama burns had not healed, he was forced to give up because of a broken drive shaft. And when Beltoise's Matra broke its transmission, Jochen moved up to sixth, although lapping quite 'slowly' at around 1 minute 26 seconds and 1 minute 27 seconds. From the start he had left the pace to Stewart and Brabham. 'I drove like a chauffeur, apart

In the pits at Zandvoort, 1969

The Lotus team: Colin Chapman (centre) with mechanics Eddie and Herbie behind him

Maurice Phillippe and the world championship winning Lotus 72

Monaco, his Biggest Success

from the fact that my brakes were not very good with full tanks; they improved as the car got lighter.' Amon had crushed a Coca-Cola bottle and was worried about possible damage to his tyres, so he let Brabham pass him.

On lap 24 Stewart lapped Hill, five-times winner at Monaco. By now he had a lead of fifteen seconds over Brabham and Amon, was thirty seconds ahead of Hulme and Pescarolo, and thirty-two ahead of Rindt; then an ominous misfire sounded what seemed like a requiem for Jackie's engine: he had the transistor box changed and restarted, hopelessly delayed, but was forced to retire soon afterwards. With a sad smile and a resigned shrug of the shoulders he turned to Helen: 'Believe me, at no stage did I drive the car too hard.'

Stewart, Hill, Brabham, Ickx—all of them would fight on in a hopeless race, with no expectation of being reasonably well placed and still give everything they've got. 'Jochen's attitude is quite different,' Chapman explained to me. 'He doesn't drive lost races. He is aware of the risks, which he fully accepts as long as he knows he stands a chance; but not once the possibility of winning has disappeared. This is the first time I've come across this frame of mind in a driver; still, who am I to criticise if he feels so strongly about it. And Jochen is completely straight. It took me a year to comprehend this attitude. Now I am prepared to work with him on this basis and to enter into events with this in mind.' What Colin didn't know yet was that in 1970 Jochen would fight for a 'damned good chance' in every race!

'If Jochen doesn't expect to win he makes noticeably less effort. But he has some dynamic inner force which urges him to use all his potential above expectations, to drive as if possessed, if victory is within his reach.'

Jochen's performance at Monaco proved him to be the fastest racing driver of his time. Just before half distance, when he switched on that dynamo and really started motoring, everyone in the Lotus pits, March mechanic Pete Kerr and many others, suddenly had a premonition of Jochen's

Jochen Rindt

capabilities: instead of 'driving like a chauffeur' he went into the attack. 'I watched Pescarolo for a while. He was driving very well but he started tiring.' On the 35th lap Jochen spectacularly outbraked the Matra at the Gasworks, placing himself in fourth place behind Brabham, Amon and Hulme. Denny was having to hold his gear lever in first and only managed to keep Jochen at bay until lap 40, 'But in Monaco no-one is easy to overtake.' Next Jochen caught up with Amon. Chris's engine mounting broke in the 60th lap, letting Jochen into second place, and for the first time he began to think that he had a chance. Fifteen seconds down on Brabham, he launched his attack. Brabham countered, and for the next five laps the gap remained unchanged. The Lotus pit was in an uproar. Nina screamed for a cigarette. Jochen was one of those drivers who couldn't understand why racing attracts such enormous crowds. 'It must be boring just to watch. But for the first time I sensed the real tension even in the cockpit, became excited myself, and reckoned my chances of catching Jack to be about fifty-fifty.'

Instead of having to fight onsetting fatigue, Jochen was now wide awake. Concentration so encompassed him that he could no longer drive unemotionally. The gap between Jochen and Jack steadily decreased — partly due to Brabham's recurrent brake trouble. Jochen chased the 44-year-old 'Grand Old Man' of motor racing — who would not have been driving had Jochen returned to his team — relentlessly round the series of sharp double bends, through the tunnel and along the quayside. This was Siegfried with the Sword, and the sword was called Lotus 49. Jochen left his braking even later; the wheels locked; the front tyres smoked and screeched like they do in a touring car race. 'Neither before nor after Monaco did I drive this well — and only once as fast, at Zolder in 1968.' In the next two laps Black Jack lost four seconds; Jochen now had the Brabham in view. The last lap but one: only 2.5 seconds. Last lap: only a second. The S-bend up to Ste Devote . . . Casino . . . the downhill bends from Mirabeau,

Monaco, his Biggest Success

the old station, the harbour bend, Tunnel . . . light, shadow, dazzling light . . . at the chicane Jochen gained a few more yards; the colourful panorama had never before flashed by so fast, and the glimpse of the harbour had never been so short. Tobacconist's corner. Behind the pits, Brabham and Rindt caught three tail-enders. Brabham tried to overtake before the hairpin, kept well to the inside, left his braking just two or three yards too late and slid with locked front wheels straight into the crash barrier. Jochen cautiously squeezed through and took the lead only 300 yards from the finishing line and won in 1 hour 54 minutes 36.6 seconds the best race of his life, his second Grand Prix victory and his first in Europe. A bewildered Clerk of the Course, expecting Brabham, forgot to drop the flag for Jochen. In the excitement even Nina didn't notice that number three (Rindt) and not number five (Brabham) was the winner. All that because of a fantastic final lap in 1 minute 23.2 seconds, which according to Chapman was shattering enough to have finished off Brabham a second time over.

Stewart leapt for joy! Not only because Jochen had crowned a beautiful race with a fantastic victory, but because he had also taken three points from Jack Brabham, the leader in the world championship. Stommelen, watching it all on television back at the hotel, was left speechless.

'What a fantastic race, Jochen!' Chapman jubilated as he bent down to congratulate his driver on never letting up the pressure. 'I still can't believe it,' Jochen said.

'The most classic of all Grand Prix races, the most publicised and the most highly prized victory. Do you realise, Colin, we are now third in the world championship?' Jochen said, back on his yacht by the time a hailstorm descended. 'This, after all, is what matters most. It'll be damned hard to win the world championship. Whoever wins will have to fight for it all the way and needs luck into the bargain. It will be vital to finish whenever possible; I only hope Spa will be cancelled, for one can't drive there in the wet.'

Jochen Rindt

At the Prince's gala dinner, Jochen appeared in a burgundy velvet suit; Stewart in black dinner jacket with frilly shirt; Brabham in a blue lounge suit and rather late at that—not until 10.30 pm. 'I really feel terribly sorry for you,' Nina told him, and then instantly corrected herself: 'No, to be honest, I'm not at all sorry!'

The master of ceremonies addressed Jack: 'You really were most unlucky. In France, we have a word for it: *"C'est la vie"*.' Brabham, managing a modest smile, replied that he didn't know what that meant in English! His dining companions laughed and applauded; everything was fine again.

On Monday morning Jochen's yacht set sail for Saint Tropez. The hero exuded quiet contentment, which in Jochen's case was quite possible without his having broken the bank at the Casino.

CHAPTER TWENTY-FOUR

More than a Lifespan

In South Africa I had congratulated McLaren on running in what, according to my calculations, was his 100th Grand Prix race. Bruce seemed surprised. A hundred Grands Prix, I felt, amounted almost to a lifespan. 'Or perhaps more than that,' Brucie-Baby replied matter-of-factly. At Jarama he had finished second; at Monaco he just touched the chicane, a surprising lapse for the 32-year-old New Zealander. Not only was he reckoned to be 'the man who always finishes', but also the driver 'least likely to have an accident'.

McLaren was at Indianapolis on May 30th to see his cars receive their baptism of fire: part of his expanding interests. 'I now know where we went wrong and what we can improve for next year,' said McLaren. All this was typically Bruce — analysing, calculating, probing. He returned to England on the Monday; on Tuesday June 2nd he was at Goodwood to test his new Can-Am car, which was to race for the first time at Mosport on the 14th.

The first test run was a gentle one; Bruce had no intention of driving quickly. The mechanics noticed an unusual number of photographers, but none of these tough characters had taken a shot as yet; the only photo to be developed had to go to the police.

Part of the bodywork flew off at 130 mph; the car spun and crashed head first into the only protective barrier to remain at Goodwood, a circuit which is no longer used for racing.

It had been left there to protect a marshall's post which had not yet been pulled down.

To decelerate from 130 mph to zero almost instantaneously is more than the maximum the human body can withstand. It is equivalent to a plane crash. Bits of the centre section were scattered over sixty feet; the front part and the wheels landed 150 feet away. Bruce McLaren was still strapped to the rear section containing the engine; his limbs looked like those of a test dummy. There was no blood and no fire.

When the mechanics searched the track later in the day, they apparently found a bodywork securing pin. Pat McLaren behaved bravely, even inviting the mechanics to join her in the evening; when Bruce's friend and ghost-writer Eoin Young accompanied her back to Auckland, he admitted admiringly: 'Pat was much braver than me.'

When team manager Teddy Mayer assembled his crew the next day, he told them: 'It was no-one's fault and no-one is to reproach himself. Motor racing is cruel. But we shall carry on!' Everybody is replaceable except Bruce, in the opinion of Eddie Wyss. McLaren had allocated shares in his company to his principal colleagues; the team could thus continue in being.

Dan Gurney was contacted on holiday in Atlanta and brought over to England. The Belgian Grand Prix turned out to be the only one which McLaren Racing had to forgo; it was here that Bruce had won his fourth and last Grand Prix in 1968. Jackie Stewart heard the news in Paris, where he was busy launching the French edition of his autobiography. Nina Rindt received a phone call from England; she told Helen Stewart, and then Jochen, when he met her at the airport. 'Bruce?' Jochen was stunned. 'It can't possibly be true.' He called Bonnier for confirmation. 'No-one is immune,' Jochen told me over the telephone; like Eddie Wyss he thought there was no-one who could replace Bruce and his many talents. Jochen paused: 'I've just been testing at Silverstone and spotted a couple of bolts in the back of the

More than a Lifespan

modified Lotus which I didn't like the look of. It seems to me the rear wheels are suspended by pins only 3 mm thick. That could be strengthened, the only trouble is there's no time before Spa, where the suspension is luckily not all that greatly stressed. But afterwards I am going to give Chapman a list laying down the conditions under which I will drive that car.'

Although so far they had only modified the rear suspension, Jochen was again enthusiastic about the potential of the Lotus 72: 'Driving it is quite sensational and quite different from other cars. Even though I used 400 rpm less than in last year's Grand Prix, I was much quicker through Abbey and Woodcote. It's a pity the transmission broke, otherwise I would have got down to 1 minute 18.5 seconds.' Talking of the development phase of his new Super-Lotus, Chapman regretted he couldn't do as much testing as he wanted because Jochen 'hated testing so much'.

That's why John Miles, whose ability as a tester was a matter of some contention, held the lap record on Lotus's own proving ground at Hethel: 1 minute 07.7 seconds for slightly over two miles. This was set, not in the new 72, but in the older 49.

Two Lotus cars made their appearance at Spa: Jochen's Monaco-winning 49 and a 72; this was chassis No 01 with the new rear suspension. No 02, with modified front suspension and reinforced cockpit, as well as the new rear end, was to arrive on Saturday. Lotus contacted Soler-Roig telegraphically, and he arrived somewhat puzzled by the wording 'as second Lotus driver'. Chapman explained he meant 'as driver of the second Lotus 72'.

Before Friday afternoon's practice Jochen unpacked his fully-enclosed crash helmet. 'I don't like these helmets, but they do give you much more confidence at high speed.' For the first time I also noticed Brabham in this type of headgear. McLaren's death had showed that no-one is indestructible and had set them all thinking. Jochen had never made a secret of his view that 'Spa is stupid and frightening

Jochen Rindt

at any speed. The organisers always complain how much money they lose, so why hold the race?'

Comfortably ensconced in a touring car, with Jochen at the wheel, I covered the 8½-mile ultra-fast Ardennes circuit for *Motorama*, his television programme in Austria. At times we were touching 140 mph. 'Up to a year ago the safety precautions around this track were virtually non-existent. If something went wrong with the car, if there was oil on the track or anything else happened, one was bound to hit the embankment or finish up in the woods. One's chance of survival was slight. That's why the GPDA insisted on crash barriers being erected, and that's why we won't drive if it rains. Regrettably they only completed 70 per cent of the work we had asked for. In any case Spa will never be safe, except when we move to another circuit.'

We filmed the more important corners; eight of them can be taken in fifth gear at 160 to 190. Jochen commented on the Burneville bend (170 mph): 'They have guard rails on the outside, but if you spin off on the infield, you dive down a steep cutting'; Stavelot (150 mph): 'Guard rails outside, on the inside just a wall, at right-angles to the track'; Masta straight (200 mph plus): 'Telegraph poles with only six to nine feet long rails in front of them. Whether I hit the guard rails or the poles at 180, or whether the car is slit open by the rails, it all amounts to much the same.' There was no point in filming along Masta, Jochen thought, because it wouldn't look impressive on TV. 'People can't imagine what it means to eat up a mile in sixteen seconds.'

At over 180 mph a red brick farmhouse warns the drivers of the 'Masta kink', where they have to fight against the temptation to dab the brakes, and emerge 'feeling like someone who's just climbed Mount Everest', according to Stewart. Afterwards Jochen sat in front of the microphone: 'There's one thing I want to add: when I talk of safety, I mean relative safety, for motor racing can never be completely safe.'

More than a Lifespan

During practice Jochen remembered 'a sudden funny feeling, and decided to pull into the pits'. All the really fast corners, where the centrifugal force distorts the suspension, were behind him and he was only a hundred yards from the one slow corner, La Source hairpin, when the left rear wheel seized up.

Jochen, Soler-Roig, his wife Fussy and I were breakfasting in the 'Hotel Val Ambleve' near the Stavelot corner on Saturday morning. 'The Lotus 72 which you're getting this afternoon is the most fantastic car you've ever driven. You'll see,' said Jochen. 'The brakes are superb.' Alex asked him about the various corners, and each time when Jochen replied 'flat out', Fussy whispered a shocked *'Madre mia!'* Where did he brake for La Source, Alex wanted to know. 'I change down into fourth the corner before.' But one is frequently faster if one uses the brakes, the Spaniard suggested. 'No, you're fastest when you don't brake, because the car's line is disturbed as soon as you touch the brake pedal.'

Jochen gave Chapman credit: 'He can do everything on the car himself, work out the transmission ratios, he really is a genius. The only thing he needs is a genius at the wheel.'

Jochen found no difficulty in deciding to drive the Lotus 49. But this started another argument during final practice 'because he wants me to drive the 72'. Chapman was very insistent but added: 'I'll never force a driver to do anything he doesn't want. But Jimmy often did things against his will, only because he knew that I wanted him to. Jimmy hated Spa just as much as Jochen does.'

Soler-Roig stopped at Stavelot with engine trouble after only three laps and did not qualify for the race. Jochen was to start from the first row of the grid, for the first time in 1970, while Stewart had pole position. But, as Jackie pointed out, one never knows at Spa.

Wearing his dark blue and white flowered shirt, Jochen popped into the garage on Saturday night. Pointing to Soler-Roig's car (No. 22) he announced 'This will be my car from Zandvoort onwards. For Spa, I believe I have made the right decision because I feel safe in the 49 and it will get me through to the finish. I need all the points I can pick up.' Herbie and Eddie agreed Jochen seemed happy with the car, 'and that's what matters'.

When Pedro Rodriguez climbed out of his bottle green Porsche in front of the hotel, Jochen noticed that the Mexican Spa-supporter seemed less calm than usual. 'There'll be a slip-stream battle; Ickx will lead it because his car has more power.'

Jochen's oil temperature climbed alarmingly during the warming-up lap. There was only one thing to do: replace the standard 49C wing with a 72-type triple aileron so as to cool the oil better. Chapman managed to get the start delayed by four minutes. Rindt went off first, but Amon scrambled past him on that first lap, battling with Stewart for the lead until Rodriguez established himself firmly in front on the fifth lap. Jochen held third place as far as Malmedy, but then started dropping back. 'I caught up in the corners and was driving as fast as possible, but I was content to lie in the second bunch.' On the tenth lap, just after he had passed Ickx, Jochen's engine packed up; the same trouble also sidelined Stewart and Brabham, so the world championship position remained unchanged. 'It would have been bad for me if Jack or Jackie had won,' Jochen observed following BRM's first win since Monaco 1966; Rodriguez was shadowed all the way to the finish by Amon.

Thus the first four Grands Prix of 1970 were won by four different drivers and four different makes of car. Rodriguez moved up to third place in the championship table with 10 points, behind Brabham (15) and Stewart (13) but in front of Rindt and Hulme (9 each). Ickx, who had to pit six laps before the end because of a fuel leak, remained without points.

CHAPTER TWENTY-FIVE

Zandvoort: the Muted Victory

If the holiday-makers have to wear sweaters on the beach at the height of midsummer, if a pale sun shines without warning and if persistent winds stir up the North Sea, then this can only be one place: Zandvoort. Yet after the worries of Spa, the Grand Prix circus always feels somewhat relieved to get to Holland.

After 500 miles of testing at Silverstone, where aerodynamic problems had been experienced on Miles's car, Jochen started practising at Zandvoort as early as Tuesday. On Wednesday he accomplished a 1 minute 17.6 seconds lap, more than five seconds under Stewart's old record, although he was under no pressure as this was a private test. In the evening he phoned Nina to give her the news. She happened to have the Stewarts with her. 'When Jackie heard the figures 1 minute 17.6 seconds he seemed pretty depressed,' Nina said.

The next day Brabham rolled Stommelen's car following a puncture and lay helplessly trapped inside it until spectators, including children, rescued him from his dangerous predicament.

Chapman and Scammell flew back to England on Wednesday night to pick up some new, modified parts. This pleased Jochen: 'That new Lotus 72 is a super car; and now this applies in every respect. Above all it's been adequately tested.' Jochen liked Zandvoort; he reckoned the 2.6-mile course among the sand dunes constituted a real test for the driver, and that it was safe. Many of Chapman's new Lotus blossoms

Jochen Rindt

first saw the light of day at Zandvoort: in 1962 Clark established the fastest practice lap in the Lotus 25 and led the race for many laps; in 1967, the first appearance of the Lotus 49 resulted in pole position for Hill and victory for Clark. The subsequent premiere of the four-wheel drive Lotus 63 had better be forgotten.

'I suppose the fast bends are absolutely ideal for our cars,' Chapman agreed when he returned on Thursday morning.

Practising started in a happy mood, although Rindt stopped in the Hunzerug corner behind the pits after only a quarter of an hour. The front brake had locked and Jochen helped to push the car back. Phillippe put his overalls on and went to have a good look at the car. By 5 pm it was ready for Jochen to have another go. Twice he recorded 1 minute 23.9 seconds and then he slid off at the Tarzan curve, kicking up a cloud of dust. Locking brakes again, this time at the back. The nose was crumpled, but they were going to change it anyway.

Jochen had strained his left hand in the Tarzan incident; he had to have it bandaged. Another practice incident involved Rodriguez, whose BRM took off at over 140 mph and flew over a timing box and the heads of two course marshals. Pedro was okay. The Dunlop people asked him what the tyres looked like. 'I ran as fast as I could and didn't look back at anything,' Pedro said.

'The condition of the track is changing constantly,' Jochen complained. 'Oil and sand make a greasy, soaplike mixture and it is a matter of sensitivity and luck whether one does the right thing. Although we haven't changed anything since Wednesday, the car no longer handles as well.' Nevertheless his 1 minute 19.48 seconds sufficed to give him FTD ahead of Stewart and Rodriguez. 'It shows you, Maurice, that one should never cease testing,' Chapman waggled a finger at Phillippe. They also had trouble with the fuel feed and Jochen reported misfiring. Phillippe stripped the car down. 'A tiresome business,' he grumbled, his head dis-

Zandvoort: the Muted Victory

appearing between disordered wires. When Stewart returned from Amsterdam, where he had been launching a new gramophone record, he picked a McLaren check list out of the cockpit and read it out down to point six. 'Attach names of drivers to side of cockpit.' This had been done, and the signs read 'Gurney and Gethin'; Hulme was still unable to drive because of the burns on his hands. What with Jackie reading those check lists rather poetically and all the spotlights in the garage, the atmosphere became quite theatrical. Jochen joined in later with Bernie and Piers, who had borrowed £6 off Williams for dinner.

On Saturday morning Courage slid off at Tarzan, just as Jochen had done the day before, but this time there was a patch of oil. Jochen's fuel feed troubles continued to plague him and he spent more time in the pits than on the track. Ickx approached within 2/100ths of a second of Jochen's best time, but then a sea mist rolled in, coming from the direction of the skyscraper hotels.

Soon after the start of the final practice session Jochen stopped at the pits and exclaimed: 'It's running well; we've solved all the problems.' He went out again and lapped in 1 minute 19.23 seconds despite full tanks. 'He'll do one seventeen in a minute,' the mechanics prophesied but shortly afterwards he stopped again and the brake fluid reservoir was found to be empty.

Ickx appeared to be getting faster and faster, causing Jochen to ask Firestone boffin Colin King to 'have a look what front tyres Jacky is using.' Finally, with 1 minute 18.5 seconds, Jochen made sure of his first pole position for 1970.

The traditional racing drivers' party took place at the 'Hotel Bouwes' that evening but the Wolfgang von Trips Trophy, which is normally given to the most promising new Grand Prix driver of the previous year, was not awarded. It was won by Stewart in 1965, by Parkes in 1966, by Irwin in 1967 and by Oliver in 1968. For 1969 the GPDA had decided

Jochen Rindt

to skip a year. According to GPDA Secretary, Louis Stanley, Miles didn't show sufficient results and Courage, who really came to prominence in 1968, could no longer be considered a newcomer.

The drivers all discussed the spot where Brabham crashed on Wednesday and Rodriguez on Friday; a place where, as Jochen put it, no-one brakes. Weeks before, Stewart had asked for the wire fence to be replaced by a double crash barrier, but the Dutch said this was impossible as the sandy soil would not permit the necessary pegs to be sunk.

Frank Williams, as always on race day, activated himself and his mechanics into a slight excitement. Piers and Sally arrived in the paddock at 1 pm and Piers immediately took up the question of tyres. He was one of the last to roll down to the start. Piers handed Frank his spare goggles and his wristwatch. Frank synchronised watches; the start was due at 15.03 – three minutes late. Piers was no longer nervous but he didn't talk much. Frank gave him a casual thumbs-up: 'Cheerio, see you later.'

At Zandvoort the wives always sit on the pit roof between or in front of the TV platforms. Nina settled down with Helen Stewart, Bette Hill and Sally Courage but Jochen insisted she should stay above the Lotus pit. That's where I had my TV crew and gear. Nina unfolded a chair and opened my lap chart.

25 seconds – 10 seconds – 2 seconds: Ickx led for two laps, then Rindt outbraked him at Tarzan and immediately started to pull away. Ickx was followed by Stewart, Oliver, Rodriguez, Miles, Courage and Regazzoni, but the order of the last three was soon reversed. 'It looks as if we'll finally finish a race, and with a few points at that,' Williams anticipated after 22 laps when Courage passed seven seconds down on Regazzoni but five in front of Miles. But on the next lap both Courage and Siffert were missing, and Oliver failed to appear a lap later. An enormous cloud of black smoke rose at the far side of the track. Siffert's and Oliver's cars could be spotted

Zandvoort: the Muted Victory

on the monitor but there was no sign of the de Tomaso. Nina turned round: 'Who is burning?' I showed her: No. 4. Nina's lap chart got shorter and shorter. When she saw Louis Stanley approaching Sally Courage at the other end of the pit roof and escorting her away, she closed the lap chart and followed.

Frank Williams checked the race control. 'Yes, it is your car. Piers is okay, a little dazed perhaps, he has been seen by the car. We'll get him into an ambulance as soon as possible,' said Clerk of the Course Corsmit. Frank found Sally with Nina behind the pits: 'Wait here, Sally. As soon as I can spot Piers I'll take you over to him.' Five minutes went by, ten. Then a police car escorted a Citroen ambulance onto the track. Another ten minutes passed. 'Jesus Christ,' Frank Williams thought, 'they're taking their time.' He felt cold and started to shiver: 'Then the Citroen came back, officials got out, talked Dutch and ignored me. Finally Corsmit came over and said: "I'm very sorry, but he's dead." I asked him to repeat it three times in English. "Piers Courage is dead".' Corsmit did so. Frank thanked him and disappeared behind the box; a little, broken figure.

With a little white lie, Frank succeeded in getting Sally into the Mobile Grand Prix Hospital, where a doctor attended to her. Frank then phoned Piers' parents from the press tent and managed to say, before breaking down altogether: 'You should know that Piers died at once.' Frank was to try later, again and again, to reconstruct the last two or three seconds of Piers Courage's life: how and why the de Tomaso left the track, how it cut the wire fence over a length of 300 yards, how the impact with the sand dunes decelerated the car from 130 mph down to 25 within three feet; how fire broke out which consumed all. Piers had not had the slightest chance on a section of the track from which Brabham and Rodriguez were able to walk away. As Jochen passed the accident spot on the next lap, in the lead, he spotted among the burning debris and the scrub, which also caught fire, the pale blue crash helmet with the Eton coat of arms—the very helmet which Piers had lent him a year earlier at Clermont Ferrand.

'I therefore knew that it was Piers but I couldn't see the car itself because of the flames and I didn't know whether he was still in it or whether he had got out. But then I thought, if he did save himself, he wouldn't have left his helmet so near the burning car.'

Jochen faced a further 56 arduous laps on a track whose conditions changed constantly, knowing all the time that his first Lotus 72 victory wasn't going to bring him any joy. 'I think I would have found it difficult to battle it out had anyone caught up with me; if I hadn't been leading by such a margin I would have seriously considered calling it a day.' Unmoved, Jochen noted a pit signal announcing that Stewart was now in second place, as Ickx had had to stop for a tyre change. 'Sometimes I think that the Lotus 72 really is a super car, and that my problems are not technical but just human ones.' Thus Rindt won his third Grand Prix, with Stewart in second place exactly thirty seconds behind. During his slowing down lap Jochen stopped at the scene of the accident to ask about Piers; the area was now closed to spectators.

In the pits he went straight up to Bernie: 'He is dead?' Jochen handed Bernie his helmet. When he mounted the victor's rostrum he let them drape the laurel wreath around him without any sign of emotion — in bizarre contrast to the bustling of the officials and of Chapman and Phillippe, who were excited about his win.

My TV assistants helped Jochen climb onto the pit roof: he appeared remote from this world, but composed. 'That somebody is lost in this sport of ours is nothing new,' he said, 'but it is bitter indeed when it happens to be your friend.'

Nina accompanied Sally to her hotel; she didn't even know that Jochen had won. The lap of honour and prize distribution were dispensed with; the PA system asked spectators to leave the track quietly. The same evening Sally was flown back to England by private plane, accompanied by Jochen, Bernie and Nina. Jochen tried to solve his

Monte Carlo, 1970: Rindt takes Pescarolo and the chase after Brabham begins

Piers Courage with his son Jason

The start of the Belgian Grand Prix, Spa, 1970. Chris Amon's March on the left, leading from Jochen's Lotus 49

Zandvoort: the Muted Victory

most difficult problem on the way to the airport by asking Bernie: 'Should I give up now or only, as originally intended, when I finish the season as world champion?' 'If you are going to stop, then stop at once,' advised his friend. 'Either/or — one thing or the other. You can't choose when you are going to have an accident, should you be fated to have one. You cannot avoid a crash simply by planning to give up at some future date. If you feel like giving up, do so here and now and don't wait till the end of the year.'

'I believe I should carry on till the end of the season, especially now that I'm winning,' Jochen said. 'You know I want the world championship. And once I've started something, I've got to finish it.'

Nina also urged him to retire. 'I can't just give up during the season.' Nina pointed out that Johnny Servoz-Gavin had done just that, when he sent Tyrrell a totally unexpected letter after Monaco. 'If I'm to have any self-respect, I couldn't possibly abandon half-way.'

His friends and colleagues said farewell to 'Porridge' on June 25th in the Chapel of St Mary the Virgin at Shenfield, Essex; just 19 days after McLaren. None of the drivers could hide their emotions; neither Brabham nor Jochen, whom Nina had never seen in tears before. At the graveside, Sally, brave and upright, turned to the designer of the de Tomaso, the young Italian Dall'Ara: 'I thank you, Gianpaulo, for building such a beautiful car for Piers.'

CHAPTER TWENTY-SIX

Clermont-Ferrand — a Win from Third Place

Jochen now found himself only one point behind Stewart in the world championship ratings: 18 to 19. But the chances of his overtaking Stewart with the Lotus 72 no longer formed his main preoccupation. His thoughts were with Piers and his doubts concerned the whole purpose of motor sport. Chapman, without blaming Jochen, saw the dangers: 'If he were truly professional in his attitude, he would realise that his driving will be affected if he worries too much about Sally. But it once again demonstrates Jochen's absolute sincerity; he regards his responsibilities as being greater towards Piers and Sally than to motor racing.' Jochen now made it pretty clear to Chapman that he would retire the moment he won the world championship.

The amusing dinner dates with Piers and Sally could not be revived, and somehow motor racing became quieter without Piers. Jochen and Nina flew with Jack Brabham to the Formula 2 race at Rouen, and Jochen only came ninth, even though this was one of his favourite circuits. In the supporting Formula 3 race two young Frenchmen were fatally injured; Denis Dayan and Jean-Luc Salomon, for whom a works Lotus had been entered in the Grand Prix of France at Clermont-Ferrand.

More than ever before, Jochen busied himself with safety equipment for his car: Firestone produced a 'safety fuel tank'

Clermont-Ferrand — a Win from Third Place

which was four times heavier than a normal rubber one, 'but Lotus could have compensated for this', according to Jochen. As before, these safety tanks were made of rubber, but were filled with a foam material to prevent the petrol from escaping too quickly and to retain for a few vital seconds longer those dangerous fumes.

'We were already filling our Lotus 49 tanks with foam,' Chapman reported, 'but not for safety reasons, as it makes little difference whether the fuel escapes in one or in two seconds. We hoped the foam would help the cars' handling as the fuel would slosh around less during braking.'

Chapman then designed his version of a safety tank to fit the Lotus 72 and, on the Monday after Zandvoort, sent the rough sketches to America. 'But two weeks later I was told that it would be impossible to manufacture such tanks in plastic, so I turned to a firm in England. They would produce it for me by Monza.'

Firestone showed their film about safety tanks at Clermont-Ferrand, demonstrating that even an explosion would only deform but not burst the tank. Of the Formula 1 constructors only Brabham and Tauranac went to see the film; Pete Kerr thought the reason for this was that 'they all forget very quickly what they want to forget'. Chapman on the other hand stated that 'we at Lotus have already seen the film'.

Jochen's solo performance at Zandvoort recalled for Lotus the situation which applied during the Clark era: 'We have the best car and we must therefore win provided we have no engine trouble, and provided tyre and weather conditions are normal; we can lose races by dropping out but we can't be beaten.' Chapman was delighted with the situation but added thoughtfully: 'It could be worrying because one may start believing one is bound to win.'

'For Brands Hatch we shall be mounting the roll bar directly to the monocoque frame instead of to the engine,' mechanics Herbie and Eddie told Jochen. 'The car is becoming safer all the time.'

Jochen Rindt

Depressed with his thoughts about Piers and worried about his car sickness of the previous year, Jochen started practising on the mountainous Clermont-Ferrand circuit, so similar in many ways to the Nürburgring. Chapman installed a generator-driven blower in the pits to cool the brake discs whenever the Lotus stopped. This procedure took just a couple of minutes. Jochen changed from his fully enclosed helmet to an open, dark green one just after three o'clock and then pressed on. At 3.20 he stopped again, holding a handkerchief to his mouth. Chapman fetched Nina, telling her that Jochen had been hurt.

Driving immediately ahead of Jochen, Beltoise's car had kicked up a piece of rock the size of a fist; it had hit Jochen on the right cheek. They stuck on a plaster in the first-aid tent. 'Jochen was damned lucky,' Herbie thought; Dick Scammell retrieved the rock from the cockpit; Jochen just shrugged his shoulders. Patiently he tolerated the inevitable photos: the Zandvoort victor with a swollen face. But then he settled in the cockpit, concentrating on the practice laps ahead: eyes focused into the distance, face expressionless.

One photographer squatted right next to the car, his camera held in readiness close to Jochen's face, while a journalist not normally known to take photographs prepared to take a shot of the scene. It reminded one of an animal being provoked in his cage. Jochen made an automatic gesture, without ever touching the camera, which nevertheless led to a story of 'CAMERA KNOCKED OUT OF PHOTOGRAPHER'S HAND' — with photographic evidence. When I later told Jochen this little story, of which he wasn't even aware, he was concerned, almost hurt: 'Most people just don't appreciate what a burden this whole driving business represents for me at the moment. Not because I am winning, but because of the accidents.' And he wondered about the behaviour of some people, 'who, all said and done, indirectly live off me'.

Another person who tried to film Jochen at Clermont-

Clermont-Ferrand — a Win from Third Place

Ferrand was Jacqueline Beltoise, which earned her a reproving if friendly 'But, Jacqueline . . .' from Nina. 'Jean-Pierre drove here with a black eye last year,' she added. Alex Soler-Roig, being a surgeon's son, later had a look at Jochen's cut and decided it needed four stitches. Alex attended to it himself in the Mobile Grand Prix Hospital. 'Now I can't eat much, and I can laugh even less,' Jochen said while waiting for Chapman. Then he left, on his own, for Royat, where a sign greeted him at the entrance to the town: 'COME TO THE HEALTHY AUVERGNE'.

Having managed to achieve only twelfth best time on the Friday, Jochen was pleased to find a considerably better set up car waiting for him next morning. 'Time is getting short,' Chapman urged. 'Get in.' With a lap of 3 minutes 00.74 seconds Jochen closed right up on Ickx and Beltoise; Chapman applauded enthusiastically, as it showed an improvement in Jochen's time of four and a half seconds. During the final practice period Rindt, encouraged by Chapman's 'minus' signals, broke the three-minute barrier, one of six pilots to do so. But he refused to take part in the chase for split seconds which developed in the last half-hour. 'We won't attempt to drive any harder; let's see what happens in the race.' Chapman now accepted Jochen's mental disposition and did not want to put him under further pressure. Rindt only made sixth best time. For the first time in ten years, two non-English-speaking drivers in Continental cars were on the first row of the grid; what is more, both cars had twelve-cylinder engines. Beltoise, the son of a Paris butcher and the darling of the French public, whose injuries in a serious accident at Reims in 1964 were expected to put him out of motor racing for ever, felt poised for his first success. But the responsibility facing him in his own country's Grand Prix worried him so much that he only dropped off to sleep at 5 am in spite of being supplied with tranquillisers by Jean-Claude Killy.

Chapman and Rindt decided to play the 'wait and see'

game. 'If Ickx and Beltoise tear off, we'll let them go.' Colin didn't believe either would finish: 'Ferrari has worries with the engine; and I know that the Matra is using too much fuel—the tanks aren't big enough and he may just come to a stop for lack of fuel.'

Jochen at first decided to forgo the warming-up lap, then changed his mind when he saw all the others go out; by then it was too late as the track had been closed. Ickx's car suffered from valve trouble and he jumped into the other Ferrari at the last moment. Stewart touched his eyelid and then pointed to the car ahead of him: 'Watch Beltoise,' he was trying to warn.

As expected, when the tricolour was dropped, Ickx and Beltoise left the field behind, partly because Stewart, Amon and Rindt were battling among themselves and holding each other up. After only four laps, Stewart stopped to change his transistor box, just as at Monte Carlo. He then continued, to finish ninth, in what he considered 'maybe the toughest race in which I ever drove': the true professional.

Rindt, having passed Amon, was now lying third, ten seconds behind the duelling, record-breaking Ickx and Beltoise. After 15 laps Ickx dropped back behind Beltoise with a rough sounding engine, and a lap later he was passed by Rindt. His engine spluttering, Ickx pulled into the pits and climbed out dejectedly: 'Valve trouble.'

Jochen now received the signal *'Place* 2, *minus* 13, *plus* 4'. 'I've been driving like a chauffeur up to now,' he reflected, and immediately started to lap faster than Beltoise, the leader. Then he eased off slightly. 'Clermont is one of the most difficult tracks anywhere; I know what physical demands it makes and how much it will take out of me. I was thinking of last year, and I know that I must try to conserve my strength.'

Beltoise increased his lead to seventeen seconds. To lead a Grand Prix, Jean-Pierre found 'indescribably formidable'; the spectators were by now convinced that his 'dream in blue'

Clermont-Ferrand — a Win from Third Place

was about to come true. It was common knowledge that Beltoise tended to slow down half-way through most races; Ron Tauranac believed it was due to the Frenchman's earlier arm injuries. But today, it seemed, Beltoise was able to hang on and to drive himself even harder.

Behind him Jochen was coolly assessing his chances: should he keep going steadily, assuming that the Matra would have trouble—or should he attack? 'The Matra V-12 was faster, but this was counteracted by the fantastic road-holding of the Lotus. Ever since Monte Carlo, I had become aware that I could worry any driver simply by appearing in his rear view mirror. I thought it would also be interesting psychologically to observe how Beltoise would react to his pit signals if I started catching up; twelve seconds at half-distance is by no means a safe lead.' Jochen's 21st lap was completed in 3 minutes 00.86 seconds, a new lap record, which brought him to within nine seconds of Beltoise. But any difficult decision as to what he ought to do was now taken out of Jochen's hands. Not only were there signs of oil leaking out of the back of the Matra, but Beltoise had a more serious problem: the right rear tyre was losing air.

By lap 24 Jochen had closed to within five seconds; he passed the Matra on the next lap, and so did Amon. Beltoise limped into the pit, had both his rear tyres checked and asked, impatiently and disappointedly: 'What's my position?' The Matra mechanic turned away. 'Sixth,' he whispered. '*Alors*, why don't you say so?' Jean-Pierre demanded as he tore back into the race, now lying tenth. As Chapman had foretold, he was to stop again three laps from the end to refuel, and finished a most unlucky thirteenth.

For Rindt, now firmly in the lead, there remained only one problem: Amon. 'His March gets through the fast corners flat out, while I have to lift. But Chris has one failing, and I think it may be this which makes him lose most duels. When following another car he is presumably driving on the limit, so that he has nothing left for overtaking. I therefore de-

Jochen Rindt

cided to drive in such a way as to demoralise him psychologically speaking; with two fast laps to get away from him I increased my lead to seven seconds, and with that Amon gave up trying.'

Jochen thus swept to his fourth Grand Prix victory, and his third in 1970, with a lead of 7.61 seconds and with a total elapsed time of 1 hour 55 minutes 57 seconds.

The photographer and the reporter involved in Friday's incident felt confounded and frustrated by Jochen's 'gift' win; after all, he had done nothing other than play his cards right. Champagne literally poured over Jochen who turned to Nina: 'If I had won here last year it would have made me very happy, but now it matters little.' One journalist, quite brutally, asked him why he didn't feel sick this year. 'Because so far I haven't suffered any concussion this year,' Jochen replied tersely.

With his points total now increased to 27, eight more than Brabham and Stewart, Jochen led the world championship for the first time. Sitting in the Firestone caravan that evening we decided on our joint book. I asked him whether he still intended to retire at the end of the year. Tired, exhausted, Jochen nodded: 'Yes. Remember how close the practice battle was, how many of us were bracketed by just one second over this three-minute circuit; all those new drivers—Stommelen, Giunti, Cevert, Peterson and Regazzoni—are going to be terrific in 1971.' Jochen wasn't only thinking about his own future but that of his sport as well.

'I'm going to try my hardest to win this world championship. This means I shall be content to finish some races in second or third place rather than risk everything for a win. Lotus are now working as a team and all their efforts are concentrated upon me; it is now quite clear that the 72 is a sensational car.'

For some time Jochen was under the firm impression that his lap times were five seconds slower than the previous year. When I convinced him that he actually lapped some

Clermont-Ferrand — a Win from Third Place

six seconds faster than in the 49 he appeared quite puzzled; but it enabled a fairer assessment to be made both of Rindt the driver and of the Lotus 72; up to then the potential of neither had been fully exploited.

'What the Lotus 72 needs is an undulating and somewhat bumpy surface; I know a circuit to which the car will be ideally suited and one which I like much better than Clermont: Brands Hatch,' Jochen said, in anticipation of his next event.

CHAPTER TWENTY-SEVEN

Brands Hatch:
Two Failures, Two Successes

Chapman, faced with Jochen's intention of retiring, had to start thinking ahead to 1971; accordingly he recruited the 23-year-old Emerson Fittipaldi. The Brazilian's successes in Formula Ford and Formula 3 led Chapman to think in terms of 'a second Stewart'. Declining the offer of a three-year contract, he instead accepted a two-year one, 'because no-one can tell what might happen'. The British Grand Prix was to be his baptism of fire; his father, a TV commentator, arranged to transmit it directly to Brazil by Telstar at a cost of £11,000. During testing at Silverstone Fittipaldi did 1 minute 22.6 seconds, not all that far behind Rindt's 1 minute 21.8 seconds and Miles's 1 minute 22.1 seconds.

The whole of England seemed to be involved with Rindt and Austria during Grand Prix week. Miss World, herself Austrian, was flown to Hethel for Jochen to interview her on television. Lotus press officer Malcolm Ginsberg gave away ties imprinted *Threefold Winner of the Constructor's Championship* by the dozen, 'because we'll have to have new ones made this year'. Jochen was happy with Lotus and satisfied with the car. Once you start winning, you acquire confidence, which you need; the less you think, the faster you go. That's why winning is better than anything else, according to an old race drivers' maxim.

During the days which Jochen and Nina spent in Chap-

Brands Hatch: Two Failures, Two Successes

man's house another problem raised its head. Nina could neither overcome Piers' loss nor stifle her concern for Jochen. 'Don't always look so sad, Nina,' Jochen often reproached her. 'I don't like this racing business,' his wife told him. 'I'm only coming along because of you.'

While Jochen left the final decision to her, Colin gave her some sound advice: 'He won't have any time for you during practice and during the race, but afterwards he'll need you all the more. A racing driver's reactions after crossing the finishing line are predictable. Should he have lost, he'll need his wife to protect him from all the nonsense which happens afterwards; to console him and to demonstrate that he is not alone, for a driver who has been unsuccessful is convinced that he hasn't got a single friend in the world. If, on the other hand, he has won, and is being adulated and congratulated, then he needs his wife to share it all with him, because it is a fact that no-one likes celebrating alone.'

Chapman was not surprised Nina didn't enjoy motor racing 'after the difficult times she's been through. Admittedly she knew the atmosphere from her father's racing days, but at that time there was none of this terrible pressure on Grand Prix racing. Even at Cooper's nobody expected Jochen to win, while at Brabham's the engine made this impossible. At Lotus, everyone expects him to be first.' And so, at Brands Hatch, Nina was once again sitting bravely in the pits.

When I visited Jimmy Clark's mother in Scotland just before the British Grand Prix she said she very much hoped Jochen would win: 'After all, he is carrying the Lotus flag.' Jochen certainly upheld it during the first practice period: his 1 minute 24.8 seconds left all his rivals behind by at least 0.8 seconds. 'Don't touch the car, it's bloody marvellous!' Jochen said to Chapman, grinning all over. 'Tomorrow, we shan't even have to practise, shall we?' Colin took it seriously: 'For Heaven's sake, Jochen, don't let's be complacent! We could have the most diabolical troubles tomorrow.'

And Jochen was to have them. In spite of every effort he

Jochen Rindt

could not get within two seconds of his previous best time. For one thing, the track was by now greasy with oil, which the Firestones didn't like half as much as the Brabham's Goodyear G24s, which were specially developed for oily track surfaces. 'I simply can't go any faster and we can't find the reason for it.' He was further delayed by a split petrol tank; shortly before the end of practice, the mechanics also discovered a defective shock absorber.

'Isn't your 1 minute 24.8 seconds of yesterday sufficient for those hundred bottles of champagne?' Beltoise wanted to know. Jochen smilingly asked his Clermont rival whether he'd like them. He was much too slow, Jean-Pierre said. Bette Hill thought the whole lot ought to go to Jackie Oliver, who had got married on Wednesday. 'I don't seem to have drunk champagne for ages,' Jochen said in toasting Nina. Suddenly Jack Brabham appeared, looking pleased with himself: he had equalled Jochen's fastest time on his final practice lap.

'This is going to be a repetition of our 1966 Formula 2 battle,' Jochen predicted, 'except that it will be eighty laps instead of forty. Brands Hatch is just as tiring as Monte Carlo; there's no place where you can relax; you have to concentrate all the way round the circuit.'

Ickx had joined Rindt and Brabham in the first row; the March cars didn't seem happy with the up-and-down nature of Brands Hatch and occupied only 8th, 9th, 13th, 14th, 17th and 20th places on the grid. New recruit Fittipaldi asked his boss what time he would appear on race day. It would depend on the air traffic, Colin replied as he climbed into his Navajo. Jochen nudged me: 'Now you'll see how a large aeroplane takes off from a small airfield. He is quite mad; you should have seen him land this morning. . . .'

Race day dawned overcast, as the practice days had done, but Chapman's prayers for rain stayed unanswered. Amon started with 43 gallons of petrol on board, Jochen with only 39; Ickx led initially, pursued by Brabham and Rindt, to-

Brands Hatch: Two Failures, Two Successes

gether for the third time in the opening phases of a Grand Prix.

After six laps the Ferrari coasted to a halt at the back of the pits with a broken differential bearing; just before this Rindt had passed Brabham at Paddock Bend, and as Ickx slowed he took the lead. The Lotus and the Brabham looked like a couple of fighter planes as they towed each other past Surtees, Hill, Gurney and Amon, who were battling for seventh place. And all the time Black Jack was tigering his way closer and closer to Rindt, who had to summon all his reserves of nervous energy to keep Brabham at bay.

'The longer the race lasted the more slippery the track was getting and the more difficult it became for me to stay in front of Brabham.' Twelve laps from the end Jochen had 'a moment' at Clearways and Brabham, coolly awaiting his chance, nipped through. With a record lap of 1 minute 27.0 seconds (1.1 seconds quicker than Jochen's best race lap) he started drawing away. Meantime the Lotus's handling was getting worse and worse.

'I never attempt to control Jochen during a race. I give no instructions as to whether he should drive slower, faster or steadily,' said Chapman, who has always adhered to this policy. 'By giving lap times and the number of seconds he is behind or in front of the nearest runners, he receives all the information he requires. His pace remains the driver's decision. I push no-one, for I could never forgive myself if this resulted in an accident.'

Anyway, Rindt showed tactical maturity. He realised that his tyres would not permit him to hang on to Jack. He therefore made no attempt to do so and drove for a safe second place; as Hulme, under strong attack from Regazzoni, was more than a minute behind, there was no need for haste. Jack had now left Jochen by some fifteen seconds and was well on the way to his fourth British Grand Prix victory.

Bernie Ecclestone ran over to the Brabham pit to offer his congratulations, but the second hands on their watches were running on during this last lap; Brabham noticed the first engine splutterings a few corners earlier, and at Stirling's Bend he ran out of fuel. Jochen saw the blue and yellow car coasting along, overtook it at Clearways and won his fifth Grand Prix in 1 hour 57 minutes .02 seconds. He still couldn't believe it. 'Oh no!' groaned the agonised public, almost in unison, as Brabham rolled over the line 32.9 seconds later. Bernie was the first at Jack's side: 'We feel disgusted, and I really mean that.'

If one leads an 80 lap race from the 7th to the 68th tour, then one has hardly stolen a victory. But Brands Hatch was not a replica of Monaco: then Jochen had driven the 'Grand Old Man' into the ground, pushing him into making an error — while this time he had won because of his rival's atrocious bad luck.

As soon as he was able to do so Jochen sought out Jack: 'I really feel most sincerely sorry for you. It was your race and you would have won beyond any doubt.' Jack remained serious and asked: 'I hope that with you, at least, everything went well?' 'Not quite,' Jochen replied, frankly. Ron Tauranac accepted full blame for the fuel shortage; he thought he might have miscounted and filled up with only seven instead of eight drums.

Jack sat pondering in his transporter; without resentment but with a nostalgic sadness in his eyes. For the first time ever his disappointment showed.

His sons Geoffrey, Gary and David squatted behind him; on his left sat his wife Betty and to the right his father, the 75-year-old greengrocer from Sydney. 'I only wish I had brought a small tin of petrol with me from Sydney,' Brabham senior said into my microphone. The transporter rocked with laughter and the sad look disappeared from Jack's eyes, although he said: 'I suppose I shall have to give up all thought of beating Jochen to the title this year.'

In the Gold Leaf tent Chapman was cheerfully sorting out the crates of champagne. 'Take one crate over to Firestone,

Brands Hatch: Two Failures, Two Successes

and one to Brabham,' Jochen said. 'Jack, the poor so and so, must feel absolutely desperate.'

Lady Luck, who refused her favours for so long, and who only smiled at him during this one short, hot summer, now irritated Jochen. 'I'm beginning to worry about this luck, because I know only too well how quickly it can turn back into misfortune. And I certainly have been lucky this summer.'

The devils weren't just painted on the walls; at 6.30 pm they appeared in person in the Lotus camp in the shape of the scrutineers, who reminded one in their over-eagerness of elderly greyhounds; above all, they were tough with Chapman. Rindt was disqualified, they announced, because the highest point of his rear wing was more than the permitted 80 centimetres from the lowest point of the chassis.

After two hours of re-checking, the result was as follows: 80.2 centimetres on one side, 76.6 on the other; the average height is therefore 79.9. Thus 1 millimetre saved the sport from further ridicule. There was a round of applause for Jochen, who had now won for the second time a race which he had twice lost—Jochen slipped into his car to join Nina and 'Twiggy'; even though the latter was used to arguments about millimetres, she found this dispute totally absurd. Not until later did Jochen have a chance to have dinner; they had to make do with a cheap steakhouse near Farnborough because by then all the restaurants were full.

The following morning Nina flew to Helsinki for a holiday with her parents. I went to pick up Jochen from Bernie's dream house in Farnborough and leafed through the London Sunday papers with him. 'Thanks to this disqualification comedy I've deprived poor Jack of all his publicity,' Jochen complained. 'Without this grotesque affair all the headlines would have been Jack's: "Unlucky Brabham robbed of victory" etcetera. Now I've even stolen that show.'

Bernie thought one shouldn't feel sorry for anyone in motor racing, except Jack. 'That he should suffer all this misfortune in his last year of racing,' Jochen pondered, 'yet he would still be fit enough physically and mentally to win Grand Prix races in fifteen years, when he's 59. Anyway, I've invited Jack to Geneva for three days. And Colin is coming down just before the Mexican Grand Prix.'

Jochen and Bernie swopped flying yarns about Brabham. How Jack once, when there was some danger of an explosion, turned round cool as a cucumber to make tea on a Primus stove, while the rest of the passengers didn't even dare smoke; and how, during a flight when the weather was particularly bad, he asked his passengers to 'press this button if something happens' because he wanted to go to sleep.

Rindt and Ecclestone also had their own aircraft; an 8-seater Beagle with two Rolls-Continental engines, which was adapted for their Formula 2 team. As neither of them could fly properly, a pilot was engaged: 'The Rindt-Stone Airline was involved in drama right from the beginning,' Jochen recapitulated. 'Once someone forgot to replenish the oil. Repairing the damage cost a fortune.' And now there was trouble with worn tyres. Bernie drove Jochen and me to Gatwick Airport; only one of us fastened his seat belt: Jochen.

Shortly afterwards the Rindt-Stone airliner was ready to take off. As their pilot was not only a professional but also a qualified instructor, Jochen was legally permitted to fly the plane. He had several lessons behind him and intended to get a pilot's licence in the autumn. He thought taking off was easiest. At 3,200 rpm and 150 knots Jochen broke through the cloud cover, groped for his sunglasses and asked for a cigarette. At a height of 9,000 feet and a speed of 200 mph we crossed the Channel. Jochen amused himself by throwing banana skins out of the cockpit and, thinking of Barcelona, grinned: 'Let's hope the wing doesn't break off.' Flying over Belgium, Jochen searched the maps for airlanes. Although he seemed most interested he hissed out of the corner of his

The first lap at Zandvoort in 1970. Jacky Ickx (Ferrari) in front of Jochen (Lotus 72)

Jochen after winning the Dutch Grand Prix at Zandvoort, 1970 – the race in which Piers Courage was killed

Jochen's fourth Grand Prix victory: Clermont Ferrand, 1970, with Chris Amon in pursuit

The lucky victor: Rindt leads Brabham at Brands Hatch: the British Grand Prix, 1970

Brands Hatch: Two Failures, Two Successes

mouth: 'I don't understand a thing about it, but I have to pretend to be doing the same as the pilot.'

While flying over Germany Jochen wondered why they hadn't sent up any Starfighters that day. A ground station radioed its congratulations on his Brands Hatch win. Then Mainz was sighted; Jochen became quite excited as he showed Brian and me the bird's eye view: 'That down there is my birthplace and over there is my factory.' The joystick and the factory: never before had Jochen, in his blue jersey shirt and brown flecked trousers, reminded me so much of Jonas Cord, the Harold Robbins character from *The Carpetbaggers*. But he was not one of the never-to-be-satisfied: the Beagle was to be sold shortly and this flight was to be our last but one. 'Private aircraft are for multi-millionaires only, and I shall have to cut down somewhat next year when I shan't be driving any more.'

When Vienna control came in, Brian suggested Jochen should answer his countrymen personally. But instead of coming out with all the jargon about 'Alpha, Delta, etc,' Jochen asked disarmingly *'Hello, Wie geht's?* — How are you?'

Unlike Brands Hatch, the landing brought no last moment surprise. Jochen put the Beagle down professionally, but noticed later that he had forgotten to retract his flaps at the start. 'That's why we had such a smooth flight,' he quipped.

Even before going through passport control, Jochen had purchased a new set of tyres. However gay or careless he might have seemed at times, safety always mattered to him. During the summer he often told Nina 'Motor racing will be a hundred per cent safe in two or three years . . . at least as far as the circuits are concerned. In fact we've made so much progress that even now they could be ninety per cent safe.'

CHAPTER TWENTY-EIGHT
Hockenheim: for Jimmy, the Last Garland

The Grand Prix Drivers' Association, the GPDA, is the world's most exclusive club. No outsider can ever join. Its only sources of income are the annual subscriptions of its members; in 1967 they amounted to 242 Swiss francs each, in 1968 they rose to 500 and since 1969 each driver has paid 1,000 francs (£100) per year in order to cover the steeply rising telephone and travel costs, the latter mainly involving trips to inspect race tracks.

The efforts to promote safety were led by Stewart and Rindt. Both of them found some disillusionment in the attitude of certain of their GPDA colleagues: 'They are quite happy to listen, and sometimes to shake their heads, but if they have to speak their approach is negative because that is simpler. As a result little or nothing is done, which is quite the opposite of what Jochen and I are trying to achieve,' Stewart told me. 'I was much concerned about Spa, but by the summer I had reached a point where I realised I had talked too much; both drivers and organisers were tired of listening to me.'

When the time came for the Association to vote as to whether the Grand Prix of Germany should take place at the Nürburgring or not, Stewart abstained (quite correctly) after describing in detail the dangers of the Ring; Ickx did the same. Siffert and Rodriguez were the only

Hockenheim: for Jimmy, the Last Garland

ones to vote in favour of racing there; all the others were against.

As Stewart had abstained, Rindt was asked to visit the Ring on behalf of the GPDA with an 18-point programme. He feared his task might be misinterpreted. 'I hope I shall not be regarded as a likely whipping boy; I don't represent my own views, but I'm going as a German-speaking representative of the GPDA,' Jochen said, after he had realised it would be impossible to put the eighteen points into effect, not so much for financial reasons as for shortage of time. This meant cancellation.

'Three-litre Formula 1 cars, with their 450 to 460 bhp, have become incredibly fast. If there is some failure on the car, if somebody makes a mistake or loses control on a patch of oil, then the pious hope that he might not hit a tree or an embankment is no longer sufficient. The cars can't be made to go slower, but the courses can be made safer. And in view of the recent accidents, our present mood is dominated by the wish to survive,' explained Jochen.

Jochen said he could name five drivers from the previous year who would no longer be alive but for recent improvements to the tracks. Asked about the drivers' fears, he repeated: 'We're not afraid of our own mistakes or of possible collisions, but only when something breaks on the car. And then we want to hit something safer than a tree. This is essential for the survival of the sport.' The Grand Prix was therefore transferred to the less interesting—from the point of view of the driver—but far safer Hockenheim Ring. Charged with the task of reducing the 'frightful risks to which the drivers have been subjected in the last few months' was Huschke von Hanstein, Sports President of the German Automobile Club. Fire extinguishers, hydrants and other safety equipment were placed at 50-yard intervals around the track. Jochen and von Hanstein appeared on a 105-minute live discussion programme on South-West German Radio to explain the transfer of the Grand Prix. They defended the image of the sport against inane arguments like 'a hundred-yards runner doesn't need fire extinguishers. . . .'

On the Thursday it was Stewart's turn to face live television, this time the BBC. 'No less than seventeen racing drivers have died in the last four months,' Jackie commented sadly, 'and the RAC representative's only comment was: "Today's drivers are very much concerned with their own safety."'

Some GPDA voices were also raised, after Hockenheim, in favour of the Nürburgring. Jochen, quite rightly, found it 'improper to play at being courageous and to describe all others as cowardly. These voices come mainly from drivers whom we only see whilst lapping them; presumably, therefore, we have more reason to follow our own conscience.'

When Chapman arrived from his Spanish holiday villa, he was suffering from a painful stomach trouble. At Hockenheim he was forced to spend most of his time resting in the transporter, and found it required a tremendous effort to drag himself to the pits. Regazzoni proved fastest on the first day, ahead of Ickx and Rindt. This Swiss, from the southern Canton of Tessin, has the Mafia look of a tough fighter and probably corresponds most closely to today's conception of a race driver as portrayed by the movies. For him, Hockenheim was just another piece of road, and Ickx was with Regazzoni in this.

'There is not much I can do against the Ferraris, but all I need are two more good placings before the end of the year,' Jochen told Chapman, who managed to argue, in spite of his stomach ache: 'Being second is not enough, we've got to win. The title may be your objective, but mine is outright victory; this time, next time and the time after that; if we win the world championship as well, so much the better.' Colin wasn't worried about the Ferraris. 'I only start feeling concerned when somebody wins; and Ferrari hasn't won anything yet.'

Hockenheim: for Jimmy, the Last Garland

Regazzoni's FTD induced Chapman to provoke Miles a little: 'I am curious to know when my number two will finally be fastest; how about it, John?' However, Miles suffered no less than three engine failures during the weekend; the suspicion grew in the team that all might not be well with the Ford power units, particularly as the Cosworth factory was closed for the annual holidays. 'We race drivers can't just take off on holiday,' Siffert grumbled.

Jochen managed to latch on to Miles and out-slipstreamed both the Ferraris. Crowds besieged the Lotus pit; Chapman raved and had all the hangers-on thrown out. Colin often had the feeling that Jochen regarded practice as a waste of time, feeling that it was only the race that mattered, but Jochen practised just enough to feel confident of the car and sure of winning.

'Practice isn't all that important here,' Jochen said, having escaped into the shadow of the transporter. 'I *shall* be glad when Hockenheim is over. Let's hope the people at Zeltweg understand that I sometimes want to be left alone and need some peace and quiet.' As usual I kept Jochen supplied with mineral water and cigarettes.

Out on the track the slipstream battle was raging. The mechanics were lined up along the guard rail, holding out their signal boards. A shock wave rushed through the line of pits whenever the colourful string of cars tore by.

'It will only need one joint sortie and the Ferraris will have beaten my time,' Jochen said realistically. At 2.10 pm, the time had come: Ickx and Regazzoni were being strapped into their cars; ready to take off against the enemy. Forghieri sent Ickx out first, followed exactly 40 seconds later by Regazzoni. Almost unnoticed, Jochen took to the track again, keeping away from the large pack which was now led by Siffert and Brabham.

On his final lap, Ickx deprived Rindt of pole position. Happiness overflowed in the tent which the Ferrari team had erected next to their transporter. Forghieri despatched

Jochen Rindt

a telex to Enzo Ferrari which simply listed the practice times Significantly, he talked more about Jochen than his own drivers. 'Jochen has managed to overcome his misfortunes,' said Forghieri, 'and he has become a happy driver.' In the race Jochen intended, if he could, to hang on to the Ferraris. Above all else, he wanted to finish but he also wanted to win. He was now in agreement with Chapman.

From 5 am onwards 180,000 spectators started to fill up the grandstands. The August sun and the loud marching music combined to stoke up the greenhouse atmosphere. The packed masses towered almost vertically into the sky. 'It's like a South American football stadium,' Jacky Ickx observed, as we strolled through the paddock. Jochen was sitting calmly and quietly in the Lotus transporter, sticking decals (for the Jochen Rindt Show) onto his crash helmet.

A number of VW-Porsches had been drawn up in the starting area to take the drivers on their formal presentation lap; one car per row of the starting grid. Jochen drove up to Ickx, moved into the passenger seat and handed Jacky the wheel; tumultuous applause broke out. 'Jacky and I devoted this lap to agreeing on places where we would overtake each other and places where we had better not.' The secret pact between two drivers who were increasingly earning mutual respect was sealed in front of this vast multitude.

Once again Ickx shot into the lead, which he held for six laps. Then Rindt took over for three laps; also up with them were Regazzoni and Amon, Chris holding on grimly, while Siffert was slowly but steadily dropping back. 'It took me ten laps to appreciate that the Lotus cornered better and that its top speed was higher than that of the Ferrari, because I had fitted a particularly high fifth gear; on the other hand the Ferrari had better acceleration. My problem consisted therefore of not losing too much while accelerating away from corners.'

As soon as the leading foursome made its appearance at the entrance of the Motordrome, one perceptibly felt the

Hockenheim: for Jimmy, the Last Garland

crowd hold its collective breath; only when the group reached the pit straight did they seem to exhale. Any hopes of championship points which Brabham and Stewart might have held had already disappeared; Jochen was just able to spot the pit sign *'STEW OUT'*, but missed the news of Brabham's retirement 'because I had to concentrate entirely on my battle with the Ferraris'.

Millions of TV viewers witnessed the duel between Rindt and Ickx, and they also saw how hard Regazzoni worked to help his team leader. On the 22nd lap the crowds seemed to hold their breath even more noticeably than before: Regazzoni led! 'This could be tricky, because it might enable Ickx to get away from me,' Jochen thought, but he was soon back in the lead again.

After thirty laps Regazzoni's engine seized and he spun to a halt. Applause covered him on his walk back to the pits like a shower of confetti. Five laps later Amon dropped out with engine trouble; Rindt and Ickx were now incontestably alone in front.

Nobody will ever know just how often the lead changed in this Grand Prix. 'Ickx kept to our agreement and was a worthy opponent,' Jochen noted. Ickx later talked in terms of a perfect rival: 'He is intelligent as well as correct. On the whole, all Formula 1 drivers are intelligent, but not all of them are as correct as Jochen. One remembers the respect which developed in wartime between enemy pilots. The respect which exists between certain drivers is similar. Of course there is no question of us being enemies; nor can we usually become good friends, because inevitably we remain rivals. But to win the esteem of one of your great opponents,' Ickx was to write later, 'is the finest reward for any sportsman.'

Jochen had by now worked out that he would be able to pass Ickx in the last two laps, as and how he wanted. Out of the slipstream; in the bends; but not on the exit from the bends. He did precisely this on the last lap but one and drove

Jochen Rindt

'as fast as I could': 2 minutes 00.6 seconds. Ickx trumped this with a 2 minutes 00.5 seconds on the last lap of all, but by then Chapman was already jumping up and down in the middle of the track, roaring 'It's Jochen!'

'Bloody good show, Jochen. The German Grand Prix is surely the one you always wanted to win,' Colin shouted. Jochen offered Ickx a drink from his trophy; and then admitted: 'A monkey could have won with your car today, Colin.' Jochen needed forty-eight Grand Prix points before he won; after his sixth Grand Prix victory he realised how easily this was achieved. Victories normally didn't make him proud; but this one was fought out over the full distance.

With his forty-five points, twenty more than Brabham and twenty-six more than Stewart, Rindt was already being treated like a champion. Amon thought it would now be 'inconceivable for anyone to beat Jochen'. No other car had even finished four successive Grands Prix in 1970, let alone won them.

While Chapman had to break his homeward flight in Frankfurt in order to see a doctor, the Lotus boys held a victory party. Dave, who had been at Hockenheim with Clark in 1968, told me quietly: 'As always, Jochen gave us his laurel wreath. I placed it on the spot where Jimmy had his accident. I'm sure this would please Jochen.' It was to be Rindt's last Grand Prix garland.

CHAPTER TWENTY-NINE

Five Weeks

He always tried to derive some benefit from each minute of the day. In the five weeks that were to follow, Jochen undertook more than ever before, and yet seemed relaxed in a manner unequalled in earlier days. His friend Gotfrid Köchert perceived in him 'an enormous eagerness to live, Jochen is almost in a state of euphoria'.

He had reached the highest point of his existence. The world championship was within reach; her holiday in Finland had been good for Nina; he had grown closer to Natascha, now two years old; the new house was about to be completed and his business was doing well. Jochen was at peace with everything.

Above all he had recovered his faith in motor racing, which played a real and important part in his life—together with his Formula 2 team and his Show.

Grand Prix racing is probably the hardest of all sports, perhaps the hardest form of competition that exists. It is conditioned by a degree of fairness which is rarely found in any other endeavour. Representatives of many countries—team managers and engineers—work shoulder to shoulder, all striving for the same end, selflessly helpful especially in moments of crisis and yet trying desperately hard to beat their competitors, which is what matters in this sport. Associated with the small elite squad of drivers are a bunch of aggressive, wide awake and well-informed individuals; every one of them, and that includes a number of journalists, is part of the group. Once anyone leaves, no matter how interesting his new activities, this daily contact, this daily challenge is lost to him. And that's why it is so difficult for anyone to retire; that's why they all decide to stay on another year.

'I shall continue driving in 1971; we'll see what happens afterwards,' Jochen decided definitely. He had thought about it all. His income, every time he got into his racing car, was excellent; no other job would earn him as much, whether as a sport, as a hobby or as a business. But even more decisive, there was another challenge: 'How would you like to win in total silence?' Jochen set a riddle to Spaniard Soler-Roig, who caught on at once: 'Turbine car?' Jochen nodded. For Chapman, awake at long last to the menace of the much improved Ferraris, was tip-toeing into a revolution. The 600-hp Pratt and Whitney turbine was acceptable under the Formula 1 regulations and caused Jochen to look ahead enthusiastically: 'In a jet car I can win with one hand.' Nina was suspicious: 'Can you be sure the turbine will not be outlawed if nobody else has one?'

Chapman took some soundings at the RAC: 'Would points gained with another engine count towards the Constructor's Championship?' Dean Delamont's negative answer made Colin doubtful whether to enter the turbine car at Monza or to save it for the transatlantic events, by which time both the drivers' world championship and the Constructors' Award should be in the bag. Meanwhile he had made Stewart an offer to join Jochen in the Lotus team for 1971. Jackie asked for time to think; negotiations were to be resumed at Monza.

Stewart now saw Jochen inheriting all that which had come his way in 1969. He looked forward with slightly malicious anticipation to the invasion of Jochen's privacy by the world's press, for Jochen 'couldn't tolerate uninformed people'. 'Whenever he wanted me to go somewhere with him, and a reporter was expected, he suggested I should simply send him

Five Weeks

away, which naturally I couldn't do.' So Jackie told Jochen: 'Now all this is about to engulf you and we look forward to seeing how you will cope.' Jochen, who basically didn't try to attract publicity but who had some romantic ideas in this respect, tried hard to fulfil the duties of a coming world champion. But for him, all this was just a beginning.

He became very careful in his choice of races, as he was determined to risk nothing. He grudgingly allowed himself to be entered for Oulton Park and finished second. Helmut Marko wanted him to be his co-pilot in the Zeltweg 1,000 Kilometres but Jochen declined: 'Please understand, who knows if something might not happen to me just in this race?'

Marko had never heard his schoolfriend talk like this. And Jochen also demolished once and for all their old code of honour, which debarred them from offering each other help in case it was regarded as weakness: he engaged Marko for his 1971 Formula 2 team, together with Fittipaldi.

A number of times he was to say: 'I was so lucky this year that it really worried me somewhat.' For his home Grand Prix at Zeltweg, which at £50,000 was the most expensive single event in the history of Austrian sport, Jochen hoped that his luck might hold once again. Robin Herd, however, foresaw that this would be just the one race which Jochen wouldn't win.

For the first time Jochen did not seem to be irritated by the mass of people; in fact he appreciated their enthusiastic participation in his battle with the Ferraris. But he knew what was expected of him. 'Jochen looks quite relaxed, but he isn't entirely,' observed Nina.

The Ferraris of Regazzoni and Giunti lapped faster during the first practice session, and afterwards there was trouble. The technical hair splitting of Brands Hatch was revived in the sauna-like heat of Zeltweg. Ken Tyrrell had measured the Lotus 72, and after closely studying the book of rules had found it half an inch too wide. Together with Ron

Jochen Rindt

Tauranac and Phil Kerr he drew Chapman's attention to it.

In order to prevent a possible protest, Colin slimmed the radiator intakes by means of power saws and files, requiring ten hours of night work and some afterthoughts within Team Lotus: 'The old man would never go for anything like that. Mr Chapman is a gentleman and doesn't go looking for trouble,' Herbie and Eddie told me indignantly. Colin mumbled about 'Bloody people', and 'only because we have won four races in a row. Whatever one does, it's the wrong thing'.

'They all want to put me on the cross just now,' Jochen said. Tyrrell was not the only one, as most of the British constructors took his side, but he was the one who mattered according to Lotus. Further worries were caused by a leak in Jochen's right-hand fuel tank, which could not be traced for two days. On top of all that the Lotus transporter was delayed owing to two wheel changes, causing the cars to arrive late for second practice; once arrived, Jochen not only overwhelmed all the Ferrari drivers including Ickx, just back from his honeymoon at Saint Tropez, but also left everyone else far behind.

Chapman again remarked that within Jochen 'that remarkable mechanism' had taken over, because he knew that he could win. When Jochen was driven by this dynamo he could fully match Jim Clark's speed or even exceed it. But more time would have been needed to prove this point beyond doubt.

As the final practice period was rained out, Jochen's 1 minute 39.23 seconds achieved without slipstreaming, gave him pole position. But the Österreichring lacked the long straights which had allowed the aerodynamics of the Lotus 72 to show up so well at Hockenheim. 'I worry more about Ickx, but Regazzoni will be the more dangerous,' Jochen predicted to me.

A hundred thousand spectators saw Regazzoni and Ickx move into the lead right from the start, but only a few

Five Weeks

noticed how Regazzoni waved his team leader by in the Bosch Corner on the second lap. Rindt was lying third at this stage, but on lap 3 the oil flags came out and he lifted off momentarily — which was enough to lose him three places!

Jochen fought his way back past Amon and Giunti, and was catching Beltoise and the Ferraris by half a second per lap, but after twenty-one laps his engine failed. As he walked back to the pits he appeared almost cheerful, as if this had compensated for his lucky victory at Brands Hatch.

Ickx and Regazzoni completed their race to team orders without opposition; then pandemonium broke loose. For twenty thousand Italians, fighting for Jacky's laurels, Zeltweg was suddenly in Italy. While the pit roof turned into a platform for the television crews, Jochen became the target for a flying mass of pullovers, shirts and notebooks, all of which he was to sign. And he threw them all back, duly autographed.

That evening Jochen sat for some time in the brightly illuminated Gulf caravan. 'Why are you so depressed, Nina?' he wanted to know. When he finally drove off he was delayed by a puncture. He had to change the wheel himself. Later he met Jacky Ickx. 'I shall always value this evening,' the Belgian wrote. 'It requires mutual respect for two drivers to discuss their future duels, as we did.'

John Miles suffered a mishap while he was testing the turbine-powered Lotus at Hethel on the last Sunday of August. John was unhurt, but the car was too badly damaged to be sent to Monza. The same day Jochen won the second heat of a Formula 2 race at Salzburg; starting from the last row of the grid, he was nevertheless in the lead by the second lap. A true copy of Zolder, 1968. 'I like the look of your car,' said Gotfrid Köchert, but Jochen dismissed this. 'In comparison with my Formula 1 car this is just a tractor.'

His holiday at Altmünster on Traunsee with Nina, Sally Courage and the children was drawing to a close. When Jochen heard that a certain baron wanted to sell a house on top of the hill, he decided to drive over with Nina and

Jochen Rindt

Graham Hill. They drove up and up until the road ended, then they transferred to a tracked vehicle. 'This house must be a joke,' Nina said, but Jochen was already planning tennis courts and where he would plant trees. Nina told him: 'But Jochen, you can't even sit still for five minutes at Gotfrid's place—and you want to live up on top here?' 'Leave him alone,' Graham said. 'He'll have forgotten all about it in two days.'

This switched-on Jochen, talking in his Austrian dialect, was something quite new, even for Graham. Back at Lake Geneva, there followed tennis and table tennis matches with Stewart ('I am a defensive player, and Jochen was an offensive one'); when Jochen played golf, he always used Jackie's clubs, with Jackie's name on them. On Wednesday some magazine reporters arrived, followed a little later by Bernie. Everyone talked shop and agreed to launch a major project in 1971, after a plan of Rindt's and Stewart's to open a holiday centre on Lake Geneva had not materialised. On Thursday a clothing manufacturer arrived to negotiate for a line of 'Jochen Rindt suits'; Rindt vests had already become best-sellers. 'I'm not that good-looking,' Jochen smiled, viewing the reproduction of himself on the label.

Jochen was in the best of moods, happy and content with everything, when he climbed into the BMW at 8 am on Friday to drive to Monza with Nina and Bernie. Provided Brabham didn't finish higher than fifth, victory in the Gran Premio d'Italia would assure him of the world championship after only ten of the thirteen races.

CHAPTER THIRTY

September 4th

Everyone was surprised when Jack Brabham stopped practising at the new Ontario speedway in California in order to go to Monza, a race which he had never won in spite of fifteen attempts to do so. He thus forsook any chance of the $10,000 starting money (and possibly the $50,000 due to the winner as well). 'But it proves that money isn't all that matters to him,' his mechanics pointed out. 'I am driving here only because of the world championship,' Brabham insisted.

Jochen, Nina and Bernie arrived at 2 pm, one hour before the start of practice. The Lotus transporter entered the paddock at almost exactly the same time. The mechanics' faces looked grey and old. 'We've had no sleep since Monday because we had to assemble a third 72 . . . we had to spend another night at the frontier because a carnet was missing.'

The mechanics unloaded everything while the transporter was manoeuvred into its final position. 'A bloody hard way of winning the world championship,' said John Miles. Fittipaldi, who had never driven at Monza, wondered whether the third Lotus 72 was meant as a spare car for Rindt; in actual fact there was more to it: 'We've built a completely new car for Jochen,' confided Colin Chapman, when he talked to me on arriving a few minutes before start of practice, together with Dick Scammell. 'The new Lotus 72 has stronger tanks and slight modifications to its fuel and front braking systems, inasmuch as the front brake discs are now mounted

Jochen Rindt

in such a way that they don't require any cooling by external means while stopped at the pits.'

The general idea was for Fittipaldi to run the car in and set it up for the Monza circuit. Subsequently Jochen would try it out for a few laps to decide which car he preferred to drive in the race. The new, more powerful engine, of the type which Stewart, Brabham and Hulme had also received, would then be built into whichever car Jochen selected. None of this seemed to bother Jochen very much; he could leave the decision until Saturday.

Chapman would have preferred him to drive the car with the detail improvements, 'precisely because it is a new car', rather than the older car, which took him to victory at Zandvoort, Clermont-Ferrand, Brands Hatch and Hockenheim.

The first thing Jochen and Colin noticed at Monza was the fact that Stewart and Hulme were driving without rear wings. In 1968, when he ran 'wingless', Hulme had achieved a great tactical Monza victory. Stewart and Rindt had both raced without wings in 1969, and Jochen felt that 'the wingless Lotus handled better than the wingless Matra' in that year.

Stewart tried both the March and the new Tyrrell, which had been developed secretly since the beginning of the year, but wasn't publicly revealed until after Zeltweg.

'I can drive the March on the limit, even get it into a slide in the Curva Grande, but the Tyrrell I don't yet drive flat out,' Jackie told me. His next lap in the Tyrrell he completed by running from the Parabolica back to the pits on foot!

It was said the fuel feed had packed up; in reality the steering swivel pin had broken while Stewart was braking from nearly 200 mph. 'But we have had diabolical trouble with the fuel system as well,' conceded designer Derrick Gardner.

Jackie's team mate Francois Cevert spun right through the Ascari Curve at about 170 without hitting anything. 'It didn't

Hockenheim and Jochen's last victory: the German Grand Prix, 1970

Jochen Rindt and Colin Chapman

The lake at Geneva
Graz, 11th September, 1970: Graham Hill and Jack Brabham

September 4th

bother me; I soon forgot about it,' said Cevert, putting a brave face on things. But at night, when he remembered the spin, he found he couldn't get to sleep at all.

Jochen finished the first practice session in 22nd place; with 1 minute 29.97 seconds he was more than five seconds behind the fastest at that time: Jacky Ickx. Calculations made three weeks earlier at Zeltweg showed the Ferrari to be 10 mph faster on top speed than the Lotus 72. The reason why Jochen couldn't get down to any reasonable time was to be found in the fuel system. The engine didn't pull properly; after a change of plugs this worry was removed in time for the start of the second practice session.

More important still, Jochen and Colin had decided to follow Stewart's and Hulme's idea, which other drivers had also adopted in the meantime: the triple rear wing was dismounted and the Lotus 72 looked oddly naked. But the experiment was worthwhile. 'It is absolutely incredible,' Chapman remembered Jochen saying. 'The car is almost 800 rpm faster on the straight without wings; I can reach the rev limit almost anywhere around the track.' This meant that it would be necessary to fit much higher gear ratios, but this could only be done for Saturday's practice.

'Without wings I shall easily beat 1 minute 26 seconds,' Jochen reported when he returned to the pits, 'and I will be able to do this without a tow.'

At this Chapman decided to remove the wings from Miles's car, but a lap later his number two returned to the pits and asked his mechanics to refit them. 'The car twitches all over the place and won't run straight.' While Miles complained about this unsteady handling, Jochen had observed nothing of the kind.

'Is everything OK—without the wing?' Bernie Ecclestone asked him. 'Yes,' nodded Jochen, 'no problem at all.'

Jochen must have been one of the best development drivers of 1970; after five or six laps he was able to analyse the behaviour of his car. Jochen didn't notice any problems as a result of leaving off the wings, otherwise he would certainly have suggested some modifications.

The new Lotus which Fittipaldi was to run in was not ready until towards the end of Friday's practice. The Lotus 72, over 10 mph faster than the 49 thanks to its aerodynamic qualities, caused Fittipaldi, driving a 72 for the first time, to make a serious mistake resulting in a nasty crash in the Parabolica.

'I was following Giunti's Ferrari and spotted Surtees, about to pass us, in my mirror. I moved over to let him through; when I looked up again, I saw the seemingly enormous rear of the Ferrari loom right in front of me. Giunti braked properly; I didn't. The wheels locked and I went straight on, over the sand, over the bank and into the trees. It was entirely my fault,' Fittipaldi admitted. Chapman was seen to have an agitated talk with his South American recruit. The Lotus mechanics had another night's work ahead of them.

As always after practice, I rendez-voused with Jochen in the Lotus transporter for a radio interview. 'I haven't got the really fast engine in my car yet, but the one from Oulton Park,' Jochen confirmed. 'But they're going to fit the new engine tonight and it's supposed to be particularly good. Unfortunately we still have some difficulties with the petrol feed, and the gear ratios were much too low. But I have every confidence for tomorrow.' We spoke about magical lap times. 'With the right slipstream, I should be able to reach 1 minute 23.2 seconds or 1 minute 23.3 seconds tomorrow,' Jochen said. The official lap records stood to Beltoise at 1 minute 25.2 seconds, achieved the previous year. Asked about comparisons with 1969, Jochen mentioned his 'much better streamlined car'. He also mentioned the second fire extinguisher built into his car. During scrutineering at Brands Hatch it was claimed that the fire extinguisher was empty, which Chapman contradicted: 'The suspicion only arose because the scrutineers did not understand the dis-

September 4th

charge indicator system. But we are not changing the complete installation, just the container and the cartridge.' Jochen was determined to work on our joint book on Saturday morning. I felt the final practice at Monza would cause too much mental strain, and suggested Saturday evening. 'That's no good because I have to talk to Chapman about next year's contract,' Jochen grinned.

He watched while his mechanics Herbie and Eddie raised his gear ratios—not by one cog, as is customary, but by two. The speed curve of the Hewland DG 400 transmission showed a top speed of 205 mph with the highest ratio fitted. Jochen had driven faster than that but not in the Lotus 72, which had originally been geared to do 200 mph, as at Spa.

Jochen returned to his temporary home in the 'Hotel de la Ville', located at the fork of the Monza-Milan highway; the bar was decorated with hundreds of racing photos, some of them already of historic value. He walked to avoid getting stuck in the hopeless post-practice traffic.

Fans milled around the Lotus transporter, asking for stickers and even overalls. 'Their English is too good for Italians,' Herbie said: 'They must be Austrians.' They were Rindt fans, his compatriots explained, and the Lotus boys grinned: 'Us too.'

Rindt, Stewart and motor cycling champion Agostini were invited to a prize-giving on the Friday evening. Everyone was to receive an award, Jochen the trophy for being the 'outstanding fighter in motor racing'. Stewart couldn't make it because of a business meeting, but Jochen and Bernie attended for half an hour. 'Great fun,' Bernie remembered; 'though none of us knew what it was all about.' Jochen drew Bernie into a tactical discussion about his final practice and the race. As Ickx and Regazzoni had set the fastest times and Giunti was lying fourth behind Stewart, the Ferrari people were jubilant already. Let them wear their big smiles today, Bernie suggested; let's see who'll wear the biggest smile after the end of final practice tomorrow.

Jochen Rindt

'There won't be any problem getting the Lotus into pole position,' Jochen said confidently. 'I believe I can take a second off all the Ferraris.' But Jochen realised that the luck of the draw would be left to the last half-hour, as always at Monza, when the track cooled down. 'Initially I shall have to check if the new gear ratios are right; I will have to run in the new engine, and the tyres too.' Jochen and Bernie returned to the hotel well before midnight. Nina was waiting to show them some photos of Natascha taken on her second birthday.

That evening Gotfrid Köchert rang from the Traunsee, as he felt some apprehension. Nina noticed at once: 'You don't usually call us during a race, Gotfrid?' His friend listened to Jochen, in the best of moods: 'Everything is in perfect order, the car is okay, you'll see.' Gotfrid felt relieved: 'I'm delighted.'

CHAPTER THIRTY-ONE

September 5th

Jochen came down for breakfast at 10 am. Nina washed the Monza dust out of her hair and didn't show up till noon.

When Nina appeared, she joined Jochen, Jackie Oliver and his wife for lunch. It was 1 pm; the final practice was due to begin two hours later. Bernie and Jochen had agreed: 'Under no circumstances will you try for any fast laps at the beginning. Everybody is going to put their foot down. But you can leave your quest for speed until the last possible moment. If you're one of the six fastest, that's quite good enough. You can start in sixth place, yet lead by the end of the first lap; or vice versa. Basically the last thing you want to do at Monza is to lead. No-one wants to run in front of the pack and tow everybody else.'

Bernie's practice philosophy at Monza coincided with Jochen's. 'On slipstreaming circuits one could continue dicing for pole position indefinitely, and there doesn't seem to be much sense in that.'

By now excitement ran high in the Autodrome. Attracted by the Ferrari practice times, 50,000 enthusiasts had settled in the grandstands, separated from the track by a wire fence and the crash barriers; they were like tigers behind bars. Jochen arrived in the paddock at 2.15 pm and went straight to the Lotus pit. Nina thought she'd seek some protection from the heat in the Goodyear pavilion. 'If I am to be in the pits at 4 o'clock, this will be time enough, as practising will continue for another two hours,' she thought at first. How-

Jochen Rindt

ever, by 3 pm Nina had moved over to the Lotus pit.

Hulme's fairhaired son Martin kept clapping his hands over his ears in unison with the blipping of his daddy's engine. Everyone congratulated Clay Regazzoni on his thirty-first birthday. The start of practice was delayed as a photographer had been knocked down by a car at the pit entrance.

As Jochen strode down the front of the pits, wild applause broke out. 'Rin-t, Rin-t,' as always at Monza. Jochen smiled and gave a wave. 'There is no Courage today to help you slipstream,' journalist Zwickl pointed out. Jochen signed autographs, the last for a fourteen-year-old girl, the daughter of Austrian radio sports director Edi Finger. The first cars were out on the track by now. The low flat note of the Ford V8s and the howling of the Ferrari, Matra and BRM 12-cylinders accompanied Jochen's introduction, down by the pit wall, for his TV programme '*Motorama*'. Jochen explained the slipstreaming that went on at Monza; his ambition and the recently changed system of qualifying, which no longer involved the 'seeding' of certain drivers. The noise was mounting all the time. 'Do listen to it; if it wasn't any good I'll do the whole spiel again when I get back,' he said to the producer, and drifted over to see Pete Kerr in the March pit.

'Jochen will never forget anyone who helped him,' said his former Formula 2 mechanic. 'As he approached me, I had the impression he wanted me to be around, now that he was winning the world championship.' Pete started the conversation: 'Well you've got your title now.' 'You know, you can never be quite sure of that,' Jochen replied. Pete knew how hard Jochen had fought for his championship and he didn't want to see it slip from his grasp; somehow he felt worried. 'I was near to telling him "Be careful"; I suppose I thought he might break his leg or something similar, but I couldn't quite bring myself to tell him that.' Instead, Pete gave him an encouraging smile.

The last words Jochen ever spoke were in English: 'I must go.' As always, Jochen climbed left foot first into the Lotus.

September 5th

At the end of the first lap (1 minute 40.78 seconds) Jochen passed the finish line being towed by Hulme. He took 1 minute 27.59 seconds for the second lap, 1 minute 27.24 seconds for the third and 1 minute 26.75 seconds for the fourth. Jochen passed the orange McLaren just beyond the second part of Lesmo, led it through the slight left-hander called the 'Curva del Serraglio'; through the 'Curva del Vialone' and rushed on to the braking area for the Parabolica. It was here, before they had any crash barriers, that Wolfgang von Trips was killed in 1961, the year he seemed certain to become world champion.

Denny Hulme, following at almost the same speed, saw the accident as if in slow motion. 'Something must have been wrong, for Jochen's car weaved slightly and then swerved sharp left into the crash barrier,' Hulme reported to Chapman and Ecclestone. 'But I believe Jochen is all right . . . at least I hope he's all right.' Instead of stopping at the McLaren pit he had driven straight to Lotus, causing uneasiness.

Bernie Ecclestone started running. He ran so quickly that he reached the Parabolica before the much younger mechanic Eddie. He wanted to go to Jochen's assistance and he believed that 'this was the time to take a look at the car'.

In the meantime they had got Jochen out of the car. Bernie picked up the white helmet, one shoe and—on the right-hand side of the road—a wheel with parts of the suspension, which he passed on to Eddie to put by the car. The Lotus was stuck in the sand, five yards from the crash barrier and five yards from the track.

Chapman sent Miles out to have a look. When he returned and climbed out of the car it was getting quieter and quieter in the Autodrome. Possibly the loudspeaker was still blaring but one wasn't aware of it. Frank Williams looked at his watch: it was 3.35 pm—just as it had been at Zandvoort.

Lynn Oliver was the first at Nina's side; then Stewart arrived with Helen and Bette Hill. Jackie's face was drawn

Jochen Rindt

and grey. Somebody pushed a chair forward for Nina. 'Jochen is okay, Nina,' Jackie tried to calm her. 'He has only broken his foot.' 'But you're trembling, Jackie,' Nina said. That was because he had been running, Jackie explained. But then Nina saw Louis Stanley and a priest. Monza is full of priests, Jackie reassured her. But this priest came from the ambulance, put his arm around Nina's shoulder and said: 'Courage, Mrs Rindt.'

Instinctively Bernie looked for Jochen in the Grand Prix Medical Unit, couldn't see him and was then driven in a police car with Nina, Bette Hill and Helen Stewart to the Niguarda Clinic in Milan. When Bernie came out into the corridor he said just three words to Chapman. 'Oh God, not another one,' was Chapman's whispered reaction.

'You should fly Nina home to Geneva,' Bernie told Colin, who asked him to withdraw the other Team Lotus cars and to make sure that Graham didn't run either.

During this fateful half-hour, Jackie Stewart knew better than many other drivers what was going on. 'The ambulance assistant had told me that Jochen had stopped breathing and I had informed Ken Tyrrell. Ken knew how close I was to Jochen, but I am only just beginning to realise it myself. My feelings are only now breaking through. I don't know what to do, where to go; I don't want to talk, yet everybody is asking me about Jochen. Ken says I should put on my helmet and get into the car.'

Was it a defence mechanism which drove Stewart into the cockpit? Was it a means of distraction? Or was it his professionalism? 'As I put on my helmet the tears started rolling. I went back into the pit in order to regain control over myself; then I climbed into the car. While the mechanics strapped me in I started crying again, but no-one saw it because I was wearing my helmet and mask. But when the engine came to life, and when I drove off, I was aware of only one sensation: I tasted salt.' From this moment on Stewart was himself again. As he rushed up to the Para-

September 5th

bolica 'it was a different Stewart who glanced to the left and thought "So that was the spot". This other Stewart was completely without feelings, without emotion; nothing existed inside him. Now I wanted to drive as fast as I could, not because I needed to assert myself over the car, or my fear, or my feelings, but because I knew I didn't want to stay in the car for long; the faster I drove, the sooner I could get out. As I drove my fastest practice time, I felt an odd sort of satisfaction; but when I stopped my eyes were moist again.'

The same thing happened to Stewart in the race. 'I didn't want to drive, but I didn't want to give up racing either.' Jackie cried before the start; after the race, which he finished in second place, he felt 'completely empty, drained and exhausted as all the pressures of the past two days collapsed; I felt capable of nothing and absolutely lost.' Regazzoni won; the animal-like behaviour of the crowd destroyed any vestige of sentimentality.

Sally Courage happened to be in Essex that Saturday, visiting Piers' family. His brother broke the news. Immediately, Sally flew to Geneva to stand by Nina. She was already waiting outside the house as Nina arrived home. 'It all happens together,' said Sally. Herbie returned the BMW to Begnins. 'It wasn't until this moment that I realised what had happened.' He was the first to return to the factory and informed Maurice Phillippe, who burst into tears. Chapman spent a few days in Torquay with his parents. 'When I lost Jimmy I thought nothing worse could happen; that it should happen a second time with Jochen, with whom I had started to be friends, is more than I can bear.' Chapman told me he considered at length whether he should retire from motor racing, but then felt responsibility for his 800 employees and their families.

Bernie returned to England with Miles. John was shattered by the whole business.

September 11th was just as hot as the fifth of the month

Jochen Rindt

had been; on this day 30,000 people had to say farewell to their Jochen at the Central Cemetery at Graz. In thirty-four chartered or private aircraft they arrived: Stewart, Brabham, Hill, Amon, Siffert, Stommelen, Miles, Bonnier and Bell; also Masten Gregory, his partner from Le Mans: 'At least Jochen attained what he wanted – to be world champion,' he said at the graveside. Bonnier confirmed that whatever might happen in the remaining races, 'Jochen will for all of us be the one and only true 1970 world champion.'

Nina felt that 'in his own way Colin Chapman only wanted the best for Jochen', and that during the year they had grown quite close to each other. 'Don't worry on my account, Colin,' she told the Lotus chief. 'I'm not against you.'

Friends in Graz had prepared a quiet reception for the mourners. 'With the exception of Graham, I no longer have any friends among the Grand Prix drivers,' Jackie Stewart lamented when he talked to me on the terrace: 'Look at Nina, look at Helen. It's a stupid business, but I don't want to give up. Not because of the money, but because there is nothing in the world I can do better than drive racing cars.'

CHAPTER THIRTY-TWO

Epilogue at Watkins Glen

Chapman was still trying to persuade Jackie Stewart to drive for him, but feared that 'tremendous problems must be building up for Jackie at home; that Helen would suffer a nervous breakdown' and that Nina and Sally, too, would persuade Jackie against driving for Lotus. 'On the other hand Jackie is a loyal type of chap, who realises that things like this can happen in motor racing. No-one can condemn them, no-one can forgive them, but everyone must accept them,' Chapman formulated.

Ickx won in Canada. If he also won the American and Mexican Grands Prix he would have 46 points to Jochen's 45. This was the situation before Watkins Glen, the Grand Prix which was to see the return of Team Lotus.

Herbie, Jochen's mechanic, was no longer around; he had asked to be transferred to the Formula 3 team. Eddie stayed with Formula 1; as a family man he had to think about his income. And Chapman, who had 'never wanted to see another Grand Prix' ruled once again in the pit.

Helen Stewart came up to me in the 'Tech Centre' and while we watched Wisell's Lotus being warmed up she asked if she could borrow my windcheater. 'I'm cold and I don't want Jackie to think I'm trembling.' Stewart went into this, the world's richest Formula 1 race, with the irrevocable intention of winning it for his lost friend; this would assure Jochen of the championship and would avoid postponing the decision until Mexico City.

Jochen Rindt

A quarter of the way through the race the distance between Stewart, in the lead, and Ickx, in second place, began to shrink. Chapman was worried: 'Ickx is starting to catch Stewart. Never before have I wanted Stewart to win more than today.'

As Ickx subsequently lost two laps because of a pit stop, and as Stewart had to give up when he ran out of oil while leading by over a minute, Chapman, for the first time in his life, mixed his lap chart. He believed Ickx to be immediately behind Fittipaldi, who was now second, and therefore urged on the Brazilian by means of plus signals. Actually, the Ferrari driver, although catching up, was a lap in arrears.

Acting on the assumption that he had to keep ahead of Ickx, if he was to safeguard Rindt's world championship, Fittipaldi spurred himself to a great race: 'I admired Jochen; I could never replace him but today I could at least help him.' As Rodriguez's BRM ran out of fuel, Fittipaldi gained a sensational victory.

Once again, Chapman leaped over the guard-rail, jumped up and down, and once again he threw his cap into the air; but at Watkins Glen his jubilation and gratitude were shared between the deceased champion and the new winner.

During the victory ceremonies Chapman saw a small banner in the crowd. It was not being waved about but was held still; silver words on black said *Jochen lives*. Chapman, in an outburst of emotion, threw his arms around Fittipaldi.

As Wisell finished third, Lotus made $62,000 out of this Grand Prix: however, the mechanics' victory dinner took place in silence. Thoughts about Jochen dampened the spirits.

Later Stewart was to decide against signing with either Lotus or Ferrari. He stayed with Ken Tyrrell. Jack Brabham drove his last Grand Prix at Mexico City; he retired from motor racing, a decision which really dated back to 1968 or 1969, when it was dependent on Jochen joining the team.

Jacky Ickx won the Mexican Grand Prix, and with 40

Epilogue at Watkins Glen

points he became runner-up in the World Championship ahead of Clay Regazzoni (33), Denis Hulme (27), Jack Brabham and Jackie Stewart (25 each) and Pedro Rodriguez and Chris Amon (23 each). Seeing the ever-increasing points score behind the drivers' names always reminded me of those war films in which the fighter pilots chalked up their victories. In the World Championship of 1970, crosses disfigured the final listings.

Jacky Ickx composed a much discussed *Adieu à Jochen Rindt* with his father and closed with the following words:

'I would like to add—as I consider it important—that Jochen Rindt died a happy man. When, after four years of courage and disappointment, success in Grand Prix racing finally came to him, he became a different person. At the moment when he climbed into his car for the last time he was particularly happy. He had the looks and manners of a contented man.

'There can be little doubt that he remained happy until the very moment of his accident, for we drivers are always happy behind the wheel. The two seconds of the final drama cannot have changed things, for there is something passionate about fighting a car that has gone mad. Rindt would not have had even one second of fear (the excitement only comes later) and he would not have suffered.

'And even if one can talk of an untimely death, all I can say is that the duration of a life should not be measured in days or hours, but by that which we achieve during the time given to us. There isn't a single one of us who hasn't left his hotel room in the morning well aware that he may not return, but this does not prevent us from achieving complete happiness.

'On the contrary, perhaps it enables us to be all the more so. The knowledge that everything could finish before the end of the day enables us to enjoy the wonders of life and all that surrounds it all the more.' Motor racing rejects any search for blame or atonement.

Jochen Rindt

Certainly during his last racing season, if not before, Jochen Rindt had become as good, as safe and as fast as Jim Clark had been before him. But only a few months were given to him to prove this. No-one can ever estimate the further progress which he might have made, particularly as he had changed his mind about retiring. But I often saw a vision: a Jochen who had retired at the right moment to a full private and business life and a Chapman who would say of him: 'With his natural talent he could have continued as world champion for years; but Jochen didn't want to.'

Some of his oldest opponents were racing drivers exclusively. Jochen, whose interests extended far beyond motor racing, was so much more. His twenty-eight years were immeasurably fuller than the seventy-five years of an ordinary man. His was a rich, almost fulfilled life, cut off at the very peak of achievement through no fault of his own.

We are the ones who are the poorer.

The World Champions of Motor Racing

1950: Dr. Guiseppe Nino Farina (Italy) — Alfa-Romeo
1951: Juan Manuel Fangio (Argentina) — Alfa-Romeo
1952: Alberto Ascari (Italy) — Ferrari
1953: Alberto Ascari (Italy) — Ferrari
1954: Juan Manuel Fangio (Argentina) — Maserati and Mercedes
1955: Juan Manuel Fangio (Argentina) — Mercedes
1956: Juan Manuel Fangio (Argentina) — Ferrari
1957: Juan Manuel Fangio (Argentina) — Maserati
1958: Mike Hawthorn (England) — Ferrari
1959: Jack Brabham (Australia) — Cooper-Climax
1960: Jack Brabham (Australia) — Cooper-Climax
1961: Phil Hill (USA) — Ferrari
1962: Graham Hill (England) — BRM
1963: Jim Clark (Scotland) — Lotus-Climax
1964: John Surtees (England) — Ferrari
1965: Jim Clark (Scotland) — Lotus-Climax
1966: Jack Brabham (Australia) — Brabham-Repco
1967: Denis Hulme (New Zealand) — Brabham-Repco
1968: Graham Hill (England) — Lotus-Ford
1969: Jackie Stewart (Scotland) — Matra-Ford
1970: Jochen Rindt (Austria) — Lotus-Ford